Gone to TEXAS

Quilts from a pioneer woman's journal

By Betsy Chutchian

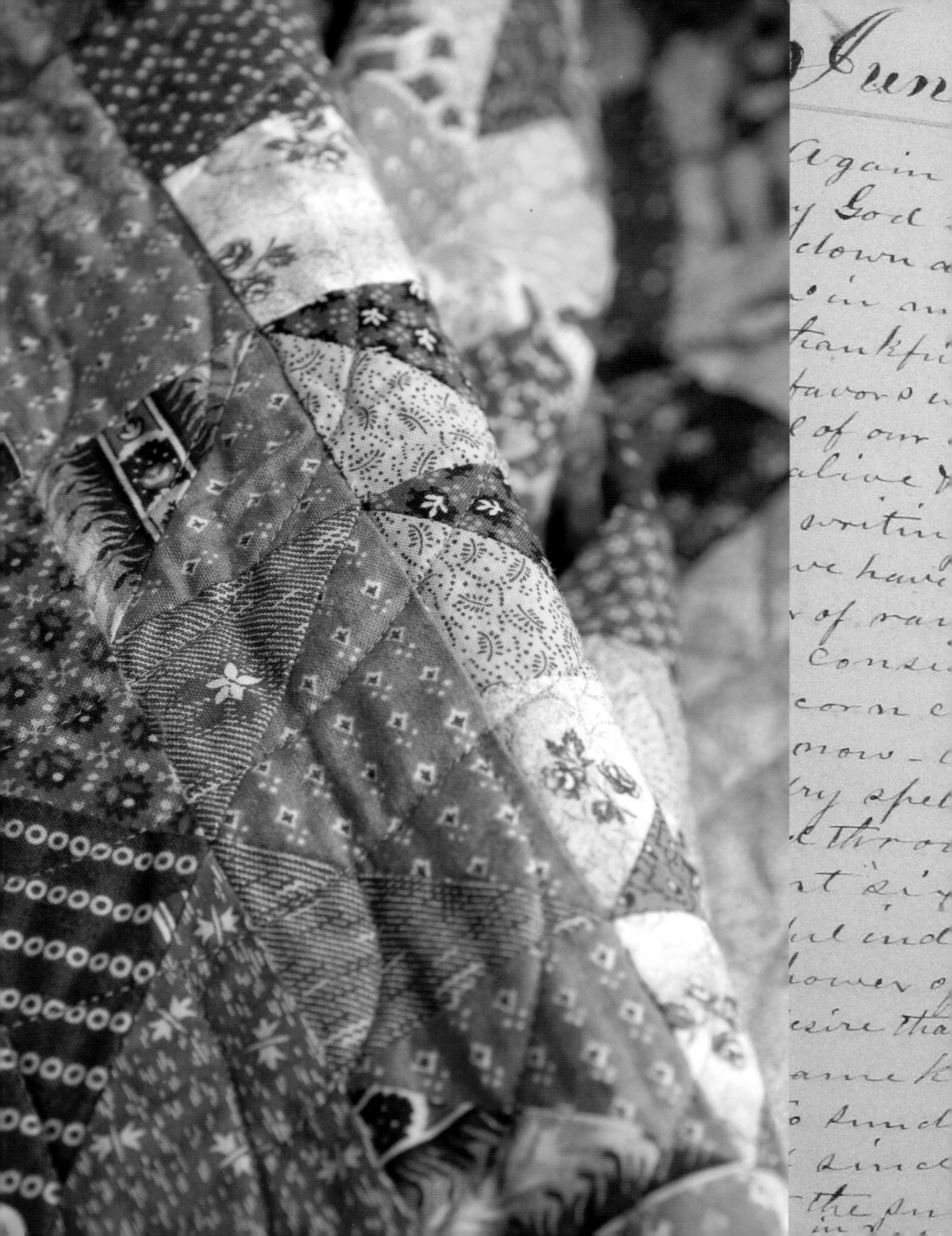

Gone to TEXAS

Quilts from a pioneer woman's journal

By Betsy Chutchian

Editor: Jenifer Dick
Designer: Brian Grubb
Photography: Aaron T. Leimkuehler
Illustration: Lon Eric Craven
Technical Editor: Christina DeArmond
Production Assistance: Jo Ann Groves

Published by:

Kansas City Star Books
1729 Grand Blvd.
Kansas City, Missouri, USA 64108

First edition, first printing
ISBN: 978-1-935362-17-3

Library of Congress Control Number: 2009932557

Printed in the United States of America by
Walsworth Publishing Co., Marceline, MO

To order copies, call StarInfo at (816) 234-4636 and
say "Books."

PickleDish.com
The Quilter's Home Page

www.PickleDish.com

Dedication:
To my mother Florence Marie Carter Reed

Acknowledgements

I want to thank my mother, Florence, for instilling in me the love of making a home, antiques, family history and good cooking. I could not have had a better teacher.

I must thank my grandmothers Ethel Elizabeth Carpenter Carter and Lena Irene Powell Reed and my aunt Ethelyn Carter Smith who taught me to sew.

I express a very sincere thank you to the women of my quilting group, the 19th Century Patchwork Divas and Patchwork Piecers, and all my students who have listened to me talk and talk about this book and given their support.

Special thanks to Sonja Kraus for her aid in piecing Soldier's Parade and Pieced Brickwork and to Marilyn Mowry, Ann Jernigan, Janet Henderson, Carol Staehle and Sonja Kraus for binding a few of the quilts. For the loan of their antique quilts, additional thanks go to Carol Staehle, Julia Berggren, Connie Watkins and Denice Lipscom.

I want to thank members of the Carpenter family who gave Lizzie's journals to the Plano Public Library for their preservation in the Texana Collection, Genealogy, Local History, Texana and Archives Division of the Plano Public Library system, Plano, Texas. And to Cheryl Smith, Public Services Librarian Senior for Genealogy, Local History, Texana and Archives, Plano, Texas.

I also must thank Renita Hall for her speedy typing skills and thorough proofreading that gave me more time for the quilts; also, Annette Plog for her computer skills.

Thank you to Terry Clothier Thompson for her loan of the antique coverlet on page 8 and the other half of "my quilt."

Thank you to the women who loaned me their antique quilts for inspiration and for use in the photography in this book. The are: Carol Staehle for the basket quilt, Julia Berggren for the Hexagon quilt, Denice Lipscom for her Birds in Air Variation (Soldiers Parade), Connie Watkins for the Half Star quilt and Terry Thompson for the Crowfoot top.

Most especially, thank you Elizabeth Ann Mathews Carpenter for taking the time to write in your journal about your daily life.

Thank you to my Kansas City Star team who took my vision and made it a wonderful book.

Thanks to Carol Bohl at the Cass County Historical Society in Harrisonville, Missouri for the use of the log cabin for photography.

And lastly to Steve, my husband, thank you for being there, all the way and back again.

About the Author

Betsy fell in love with fabric and quilts as a child learning to sew on both her grandmother's treadle machines. The beds at her grandmother's house in Frisco, Texas were covered with Depression-era scrap quilts. Her mother would point to each piece fabric and say, "that was my dress, and this was Mother's apron, this was Daddy's shirt, and this one was Sissy's dress" and so forth. In 1969, Betsy received her first sewing machine from her aunt Sissy, a 1940s Singer that she used until 1983.

In 1980, Betsy received a B.A. in History from the University of Texas at Arlington. That same year she taught herself to quilt after receiving a quilt top made by a great aunt and great grandmother. This began a passionate journey that would combine the love of fabric, quiltmaking and history. From the time she started to quilt, she wanted her quilts to look like old, 19th Century-era quilts—the ones women used every day, not the pristine heirlooms that were put away only to be brought out for company.

Betsy has taught quiltmaking since 1990 for a number of quilt shops in Texas and is a former quilt shop owner. She can most often be found at Lone Star House of Quilts in Arlington, Texas. Since 2004, Betsy has traveled across Texas sharing her love of 19th Century reproduction quilts in lectures, trunk shows and workshops. She is a co-founder of the 19th Century Patchwork Divas, a close-knit group of quilters bound by their love of old quilts. The Divas have had their quilts featured in exhibitions at two International Quilt Festivals in Houston in 2004 and 2009. In 2009, the Diva's exhibition traveled to Chicago, Pittsburgh and Long Beach, Calif., as well as the Rocky Mountain Quilt Museum.

Besides quilting, Betsy enjoys cooking, antiquing and collecting antique quilts.

Betsy and husband Steve, of 33 years, live in Grand Prairie, Texas and have two grown children, Rachel and Matthew, and three cats, Bandit, Shadow and Winston.

About the Photography

The photos in Gone to Texas were taken on location at the Sharp-Hopper Log Cabin in Harrisonville, Missouri. The cabin is one of the few structures that survived General Order No. 11, which devastated much of Jackson and Cass counties during the Kansas-Missouri Border War of the Civil War.

Just as Lizzie and her family emigrated from Kentucky, the Sharp family also came from Kentucky to settle, not in Texas, but in Missouri. In 1835, Samuel and Frances Lyon Sharp, built their log home three miles north of Harrisonville, which had not yet been established. In 1974, the cabin was donated to the Cass County Historical Society. For more information, visit www.casscountyhistoricalsociety.org.

CONTENTS

My great-grandparents, Jefferson Davis and Florence Carpenter, and family. My grandmother, Ethel, is the girl with blonde hair.

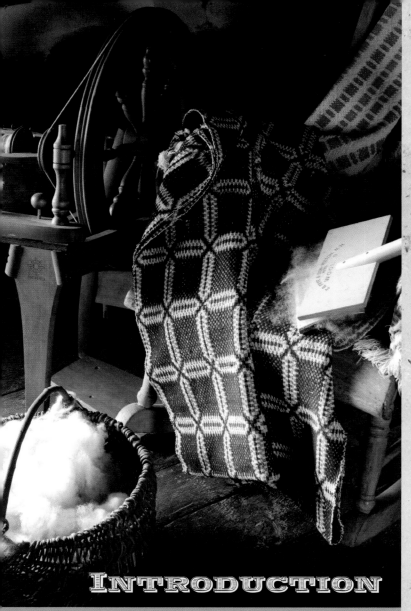

INTRODUCTION

"It's not that I belong to the past, but that the past belongs to me."
Mary Antin

Some of us are keepers of the past as historians or as caretakers of treasures long discarded. I have always felt this connection to the past in part, because of a family reunion held in 1952. It was then that descendants of Robert and Elizabeth (Lizzie) Carpenter got together to celebrate 100 years of the family's heritage in Texas. To commemorate the event, a family history was compiled which included excerpts from the journals of Lizzie Carpenter, my great-great grandmother. My mother kept our copy safe and secure in a desk drawer, thankfully surviving a house fire in 1996.

From childhood, this book held a great fascination for me as a child who loved history. This spiral bound book was filled information that was compiled before I was born in 1955, giving me a direct link to our family's past and life

in the 1800's. There was detailed genealogy and stories that had been passed down through the generations as well as parts of journal entries. It wasn't until 2007, however, that I learned all of Elizabeth Mathews Carpenter's journals had been transcribed and were housed at the Haggard Library in Plano, Texas. Lizzie wrote approximately 800 pages between 1857 and her death 1882. Robert continued the journal until he remarried in 1883. In reading Lizzie's journals, I found myself connecting with her in more ways than just as her great-great granddaughter.

Page after page of this amazing record of her work and daily life was filled with sewing and quilting references. I was thrilled to discover the joy she found in her quilting, sewing and other textile making just as I do. As I read the entries, I was delighted to find that Lizzie and I made many of the same quilts. Among them were Nine Patch, Irish Chain, Crowfoot, Ocean Waves, Double T, Lone Star and Hexagon (which she noted in 1880 was "intended for Jefferson Davis Carpenter," my great grandfather). A true testament to the everlasting popularity of these patterns.

It didn't take long for me to feel a deep and profound bond with this woman who lived so long ago, but yet was connected to me by more than blood.

How this book came about

About the same time I learned of the journals in the Plano Library, my passions for fabric, quiltmaking, antique quilts, family and history all collided in a small Texas town where I found a particularly fabulous antique quilt in a heap on the floor of an antique mall.

Hundreds of fabrics, mostly browns, reds, and purples, dating to the mid-19th Century comprise the quilt top. An 1830s quilt and two woven coverlet pieces are sewn together to make the batting. The binding had been removed. There at my feet, was Lizzie, symbolically stitched in this quilt. That old, brown quilt found me for a reason.

As I looked at this quilt, I thought of how many garments and quilts Lizzie made throughout her life and the wool she spun, dyed and wove into blankets. I also thought of how nothing was left to waste so it would have been logical to take worn blankets, salvaging the good along with an older worn out quilt to make the batting. Could Lizzie have made it? She certainly could have, but whether she did or not is purely a guess. Somehow—to me—this quilt represents her work. I named this quilt Gone To Texas. It is reproduced for you on page 34.

What you'll find in this book.

To the best of my knowledge, none of Lizzie's textiles exist today. She scalded the linens and bedding at the very least once a month, sometimes more often. So it's easy to imagine that they simply were used up, leaving no hints as to what they actually looked like.

The patterns you'll find in this book are recreations of Lizzie's quilts, as inspired by those journal entries. She talks of her quiltmaking but rarely includes names of the patterns she chose to use. It was left to me to put the clues together and decipher what her quilts would have looked like based on the era in which she lived and resources available to her.

Sprinkled among the patterns, you'll find excerpts from Lizzie's journals. Although seemingly sparse in description, it doesn't take much imagination to read between the lines and learn what this woman's life was like. It has been a very difficult task to limit the number of entries written over hundreds of pages spanning nearly thirty years.

As you read the entries, remember Lizzie was writing to her dear friend. Her words are often fragments of the day's thoughts—random and rarely punctuated. The spelling varies from month to month, including the names of her boys. When she missed days or weeks writing, she often apologized for neglecting her dear friend. Lizzie's original language and punctuation is preserved in the journal entries reproduced in this book.

I hope through reading the journal entries you see how Lizzie was just like today's quilter, working on more than one project at a time and always anxious to go to town to see the new goods.

Modern day thoughts on journal writing

Even before I read the all of Lizzie's extensive writings, I had the notion that I would note the day's events, thoughts, concerns, quotes and such, in a journal of my own. I began keeping a journal in 2005 as an extension of a class I taught, suggesting my students do the same. I would read to the class diary entries of interest written by various women as they crossed the plains, prairies, rivers, and mountains going west in the mid 19th Century including their hopes and joys as well as trials and sadness. Had they not written down their experiences, an important insight into women's history would be lost.

Much of Lizzie's thoughts, recorded on paper were as simple as the day's chores, as happy as having the young people come to play croquet or attending a quilting bee, or as melancholy as mourning the death of a child. Whatever we do has meaning every day, even the menial little things we take for granted.

Today, internet trends are toward blogs, which in essence are modern day journals. But, why do I write in a journal instead of writing a blog? Maybe someday I'll have a blog, but for now, my thoughts are just that, my thoughts. Once they are posted on a blog, they become public knowledge, no longer belonging only to me. In a journal, I can share if I want, or keep it to myself tucked away for family to discover at a later date. Maybe someday, my great-great granddaughter will find a deep and abiding connection with me as I have with Lizzie.

What I have learned most from Lizzie and her journal writing is to give details. One of my students asked, when I had complained that Lizzie made so many quilts with no details or even a name, if I was naming and adequately describing the quilts I was working on. It made me think – was I writing down the details I so craved from Lizzie? As I flipped through my pages I was happy to read the answer was yes, but I still could do better. I'll be more attentive, dear journal, in the future.

Lizzie Carpenter

Gone to Texas

When Texas became a state in 1845, many restless men and women, lured by the promise of rich soil, a climate for long growing seasons and vast prairies lush with tall grass, left their homes to start over or start their married lives and build a home and family. Before and after the Civil War, many adventurous souls came from both North and South, especially Tennessee and Kentucky where signs were left on their doors that read "Gone to Texas." Some were leaving behind mounting debts, or land that was no longer fruitful, or families and friends. Many came as a result of advertisements or recruitments for the Peters Colony, an American and English investment group that, in agreement with Texas, had land surveyed for settlement. The group was headquartered in Louisville, Kentucky and offered land in North Central Texas. In their contract with Texas, the group had three years to bring in 200 or more settlers.

In December of 1851, Robert Washington Carpenter married Elizabeth Ann Mathews both of Oldham County, Kentucky. Shortly after their marriage, Robert inherited $900 upon the death of his father. He came to Texas by stagecoach, in March of 1852 to look for land near Plano, Texas. He purchased just enough land for a home and barns, about a half section, on Spring Creek for $.50 an acre. This was close to land owned by his friend Alfred Harrington and brother-in-law Benjamin Mathews, who had emigrated from Kentucky in 1848 to join the Peters Colony in North Central Texas.

Robert returned to Kentucky, where sometime in the summer of 1852, he and Lizzie started for Texas, bringing two slaves, two oxen, a walnut bedroom suite and matching desk. Sometime that fall, they arrived at the Harrington's, with whom they stayed while they built their log cabin. Additional land with timber was purchased soon after along Rowlett Creek bottom. Cattle and sheep could, at that time, graze on the open prairie near their home. Lizzie an Robert were joined by her mother, sisters and another brother in 1857.

Together Robert and Lizzie, my great-great-grandparents, would raise seven sons, bury an infant daughter, and take in to raise three orphaned boys. Lizzie made all of the family's clothing and bedding as well as for slaves and hired help. Sheep were sheared, wool picked, carded, spun into thread and woven by Lizzie. Robert planted cotton that would then also be carded, spun and woven. Lizzie dyed both wool and cotton thread for garments, bedding, socks and stockings. She sold garments, wool and butter to contribute to the family's income.

The Journals

Lizzie kept written records of her work and daily life beginning in 1857 and continuing until her death in September 1882, one month shy of her 50th birthday. Among the details of everyday chores and events, visits with family and friends, her faith and her church, a devoted wife and mother emerges as a prolific seamstress, quilter, knitter, carpet maker, gardener, cook and more.

Comments on birth and death, sickness and health, crops, livestock, and the weather are ever present. In 1868, she began to keep a tally of her work for the year. The number of garments, quilts, comforts and other textiles that she made is astounding, but probably typical of pioneer women at the time. If she wasn't working on her own textiles, she was helping her mother, sisters, sisters-in-law, daughters-in-law or friends sew and quilt.

Journal excerpt

1868

This year I have kept a kind of memorandum of the work I did through the year- all of the principal things I have counted – but many little things is omitted which amounts to considerable in a years time as I did not count any of my patching or fruit drying or garden work.

The following is my list for the year 1868

Garments cut and made	136	
Yards of cloth wove	55 1/2	
Comforts quilted	6	
Quilts quilted	3	
Quilts pieced	3	
Cotton rolls carded for	44 cuts	
Yarn spun for knitting	15 cuts	
Socks and Stockings knit	12 pair	
Cut carpet rags for	15 yards carpeting	
Spooled and warped pieces of cloth	4	
Straw hats plated and made	1	

Most journal entries concerning piecing and quilting don't include names of the quilts. Lizzie often wrote, "Put in my quilt," "got out my quilt," "comenced old quilt" or "quilted a cradle quilt." Among the quilts that were named, are: Irish Chain, Nine Patch, Hexagon, Plated Hexagon, Basket, Crowfoot, Ocean Waves, Half Star, Pieced Brickwork, T and Lone Star. These form the basis of the quilts patterned in this book.

Colors and fabric descriptions for quilts are mentioned only once for a quilt Lizzie called a Common Calico, "plain square with red strips and yellow corners–will set together with light calico strips."

There were occasional comments on dying wool and cotton for knitting or weaving. Lizzie wrote in October 1859, "set my blue dye...tried to color a little red but didn't succeed." And in June 1867, "I colered a little wool red last week the first ever with cochimal (cochineal) – it looks very well – Mary Ann came down and showed me how."

Purchased fabrics are described when making a garment for the boys, dress or bonnet. In February 1863, she says: "I made Jeff a little pink calico apron...sewed on my green calico bonnet" and in June 1874, "I made myself a dress to day white with black flower – I made it very plain – I did not think I would like it any other way." In January 1863 Lizzie recorded paying $30 for 10 yards of cotton stripe and then on February 2 wrote: "cut out my $30 cotton dress and made a skirt"

Lizzie's lasting legacy

In all, Lizzie filled six journals with her daily record of accomplishments and observations on her life. These were passed down and kept in the trust of her children and grandchildren. Sometime in the years following the 1952 Carpenter family reunion, Lizzie's descendants loaned the journals to the Haggard Library in Plano, Texas, where they were transcribed.

The fifth journal, dated 1876-1880, was the only one donated to the library. For some reason, it was only partially transcribed and is still housed there today. A seventh journal continued the Carpenter history as written by Robert's second wife Nellie. The whereabouts of the six journals not donated to the library is unknown, and they are presumed to be still in the possession of family members or lost over the years.

Lizzie and Robert Carpenter

But the true legacy of Lizzie's journals is its unwavering record of daily domestic life of a pioneer woman. Her struggles and her joys both represented, describe her busy life surrounded by men and boys. Female visitors and visits she made to family and friends are noted in her journals happily, and regretfully noted when no one comes. It is no wonder that she sought to make her home as comfortable as possible and to add some beauty with her quilts. And, it's because of these journals that today, we can get a true, honest picture of what it was like to live the life of a pioneer woman who had "Gone to Texas."

About reproduction fabrics

Great care was taken in the choice of fabrics used in the quilts that appear in Gone To Texas. My desire was to make the quilts as close to what my great-great grandmother, living in Texas in the mid-1800s would have made. With today's selection of reproduction fabrics, the job of choosing appropriate fabrics is much easier than it was just a few years ago.

To help you when picking your own reproduction fabrics, I have given colors clues in the fabric requirements for each quilt in this book. Some of these colors and terms may be new to you. To help understand what colors were in the mid to late-1800s, refer to this brief list of colors and a short explanation the terms.

Blue

Indigo was produced throughout the 19th Century. It was an extremely popular dye for its colorfast quality because it could hold its color through harsh washings. Prussian Blue, as found in Nine Patch and Crossroads, was a vibrant blue often found in Baltimore quilts.

Red

Red can be found in a variety of shades throughout the 1800s and were also colorfast. Turkey reds have more brightness than do madder reds, which look rusty and earthy. Both come from the root of the same madder plant but have different mordants and processes to achieve a variety of shades. Mordants are different substances used with the dye to achieve different colors. A claret red, for example is distinguished by the color of red wine and was prominent in fabrics near the end of the 19th Century and was not used in these projects.

Pink

Pink appears throughout the century with light backgrounds or with another pink background creating a look known as double pink.

Green

Green is found in a variety of shades from blue green to yellow green. It frequently turned brown as its dye was often fugitive, meaning it faded over time. Blues were over-dyed with yellow or yellow over-dyed with blue to make green. A bright yellow green is often referred to as acid green and is known now on the market as poison green.

Yellow

Yellow has a variety of shades from soft buttery hues to neon-like chrome yellow to orangey yellows that we call cheddar today for the color resembles cheddar cheese.

Black

Black dyes for cotton were not stable until after the American Civil War. The mordants used were very harsh and the fabrics rotted away in cotton fabrics. Black in quilts before the Civil War would have been wool or silk and if you see tiny holes on antique Turkey red fabrics then you know it was where a black once was.

Brown

Brown was also found throughout the century. Chocolate brown has many shades and tones. They can be warm and they can be cool and they blend with everything. Try thinking of brown as a warm neutral that softens other colors and accents colors—like a black does—but without the sharp contrast.

Madder Fabrics

Madder dyes come from the root of the madder plant. Although most associate with red, not all madder fabrics are red. By using different mordants to set the dye, dyers could achieve not just a cinnamon or rusty red known as madder red, but also madder brown, madder pink, madder orange and even madder purple.

If you still are unsure of your fabric choices, don't forget to ask for help at your local quilt shop. Knowledgeable staff members will often be able to help you pick out the appropriate reproduction fabrics for your project or will point you in the right direction for help. They will also point you to books on the subject of identifying 19th Century fabrics if you want to learn more.

As so many of their generation did, Robert and Lizzie Carpenter packed up their belongings and headed West to find a better life. They chose the North Central Texas prairie to set up housekeeping. And, it was here, on their newly built homestead, that Lizzie began writing her journal, which she kept from 1857 to 1882.

Nine Patch
AND CROSSROADS

In the middle of the 19th Century, westward expansion was at its high point. Many came to reside in Texas, traveling months by wagon and on foot, often to join family members who had come before them. They came by different roads and crossed rivers to find prairies lush with grass and rich soil. Once they arrived, a plot of land was purchased and a home was built.

When Lizzie and Robert arrived in Texas in 1852, they had friends and some family already near where they purchased their land. More family members left Kentucky and joined Lizzie and Robert in 1857.

1857

December
6th is a beautiful day the sun shines warm and pleasant as spring of the year I would like to see Mother and all the folks roll in this evening for I know they are tired of traveling over these bad muddy roads.

9th made some sheets   a pair of pillow slips   cut out some shirts

15th Ma and the folks helped me get dinner

24th sewed a little   Ma moved her things home

25th went to Mothers *(Lizzie's mother Catherine Potoff Schrader Mathews Lunsford left Kentucky in October 1857 with Lizzie's half sisters Nancy Catherine and Mary Susanna, half brother Simon, brother William Gipson Mathews. They arrived at the Carpenter home in December and bought a place nearby).*

1858

January

4th cut out and made my riding skirt

5th Sewed some on my black debase dress

22nd Made Jane a calico dress

February

1st made my calico dress I got from pedlar

2nd went to Mothers cut out and sewed on my quilt

3rd sewed on my quilt

4th sewed on my quilt went to mas in the evening to help quilt

5th went to mas to help quilt

6th peaced a little on my quilt

8th finished my quilt

15th quilted my red worsted skirt

March
5th cut our some quilt peaces and commenced an old quilt   Went to ma's in the evening to help her quilt

6th sewed some on my quilt

8th finished my quilt

13th went to ma's in the evening to help sis on her quilt

15th cut out my dress, dark calico

19th went to Ma's to help quilt on Kate's quilt

20th finished Millas striped cotton dress- went fishing in the evening

22nd helped ma quilt in the evening

23rd ma came over to sack her hams I got dinner- traveler to dinner-spun a little cotton

31st a tolerably pretty day sewed some on a quilt old nine patch

continued on page 20

Nine Patch
AND CROSSROADS

1858
36" X 48"

MADE AND QUILTED BY BETSY CHUTCHIAN.

BLOCKS 6" FINISHED

Fabrics

Assorted prints in a variety of colors:

1 1/2 yards total for Nine Patch blocks.

7/8 yard total for Crossroads triangles.

1/2 yard total for Crossroads cross.

1/2 yard binding in fabric of your choice.

1 1/2 yards backing.

Nine Patch block assembly

For each Nine Patch block, cut 9 – 2 1/2" squares from two contrasting fabrics.

Lay out 9 squares as shown below. Sew into rows. Join the rows to create the block. Press to the dark, making sure to stagger the seams. Make 29 Nine Patch blocks.

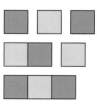

Crossroads block assembly

For each Crossroads block, cut:

1 – 6 1/2" square cut from corner to corner on both diagonals.

1 – 1 1/4" square for the center.

4 – 1 1/4" x 5" strips for the cross from contrasting fabric.

Lay out fabrics and sew as shown below. Press to the cross.

Trim block to 6 1/2" using a 6 1/2" square ruler with 45 degree angle.

Make 19 Crossroad blocks.

Quilt top assembly

Arrange the blocks into 8 rows of 6 blocks. Note the placement of the Nine Patch blocks and the Crossroads blocks in the assembly diagram on page 21. Press each row in opposite directions.

Sew in rows. Press, staggering the seams. Join the rows together. Press each row in same direction.

1858 *continued*

April 9th
scalded and scoured the house - peaced a little on my old quilt Gippy (brother) called in the evening

10th put in my quilt - Mary Ann, Kate, Ma and sis to help me quilt-a pretty day

19th squesed out my starch   helped wash wool

20th went to bens to help Mary quilt on her old quilt.

Things at McKinney

Bolt blue calico 35 yds $4.55

May 3rd
picked wool

10th Worked in my garden went to Bens to get Mary Ann to color my wool blue

12th picked wool-teribly tedious

14th picked wool   went a dew berry hunting with sis

25th cut wheat here today sewed on Willy a couple of pants

June 24th
Went up to Ma's cut out and sewed on my brilliantine dress

25th sewed on my dress

26th scalded, scoured and suned, etc   went a fishing in the evening

July 7th
I went plum hunting

14th set my blue dye

20th helped with dinner   thrasher here   very warm day sewed a little in the eve

26th spun some for my jeans

23rd Mrs Yager came to make molasses

25th sewed a little   done some baking for my sewing party cut out several garments

26th had a little sociable sewing party composed of Mrs and Miss Lunsford and Mrs Mathews and Mrs Givens

October 19th
bated some more cotton and put in my quilt-Kate to help me quilt

20th quilted some- Miss Jennie Givens to see me in the evening-Kate to help me quilt

21st Mary Ann to see me- got out my quilt

Februar

Finishing

Nine Patch and Crossroads was machine quilted in an overall design using monofilament thread as to not detract from the large variety of fabric used in this quilt.

Bind with a fabric of your choice that complements the quilt.

Triple Irish Chain

As children were added to the Carpenter household, the number of beds increased. Once the boys outgrew the cradle they would be moved to the little bed. Lizzie notes making a number of quilts for both beds, but not the pattern names. The journal entries tell us that Lizzie and her sister-in-law, Mary Ann, made Irish Chain quilts in 1860.

1860

March 1st Went to Ben's to help Mary quilt on new Irish Chain quilt

5th batted some cotton and fixed my quilt lining and put in my quilt   quilted a little

9th quilted some   Ma came and helped me quilt to day but we couldn't get it out for it is quilted close

14th quilted pretty steady to day   men hauling barn timbers

15th finished my quilt this morning

April 24th to day I worked me a collar and cuffs with turkey red

Listed by Lizzie as profits for April:
Yoke of oxen $40.00   Wool to B Mathews 5.00 and Wool to Mother 16.80

May 12th went to Plano with ma Mr Fowler's new goods came out a day or two ago

24th went to Plano to get the childrens likeness taken in the evening

29th made a bed tick and filled it up Expenses for May: Buggy and Harness $35.00   things at Plano 33.00   Taking likenesses $13.50

June 18th scalded the beds and made 3 tablecloths

20th helped about dinner   colored some red   made a table cloth

28th spun 12 cuts of yarn

July 6th spun some for my blanket

9th Made Gippy a pair of pants and batted some cotton

10th got dinner   Milla and Jane at Spring Creek washing   put some borders on my quilt

October 5th went to Ben's to help Mary Ann quilt several ladies there

12th doubled some yarn, very cool day I am 28 years old to day

Having neglected my book for a month or two I have forgotten all about what I've done, so I guess I will have to let that alone, and make a new beginning and try to attend to my business better. So I will commence on next page with 1861.

1860
44" X 58"

MADE BY BETSY CHUTCHIAN
QUILTED BY SHERI MECOM

Fabrics

1 7/8 yards cream – 13/8 yards for piecing, 1/2 yard for border.

1 3/4 yards red – 7/8 yard for piecing, 7/8 yard for border.

1 1/4 yards cheddar – 3/4 yard for piecing, 1/2 yard for binding.

3-4 yards of backing fabric, pieced to measure 50" x 66".

Cutting

Note: All strips are cut selvage to selvage.

From cream, cut:
3 – 5 1/2" wide strips, cut again into 18 – 5 1/2" squares.
3 – 3 1/2" wide strips.
14 – 1 1/2" wide strips, reserve for strip piecing.
6 – 2" wide strips, reserve for border.

From red, cut:
19 – 1 1/2" wide strips, reserve for strip piecing.
13 – 2" wide strips, reserve for border.

From cheddar, cut:
16 – 1 1/2" wide strips, reserve for strip piecing.

Panel assembly

Strip piece according to diagrams for each panel.

Arrows denote pressing directions. A full panel is made from selvage to selvage strips. Half panels are made from half selvage to selvage strips that were cut along the center fold. Cut strips from panels into increments as indicated.

A

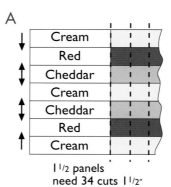

1 1/2 panels
need 34 cuts 1 1/2"

B

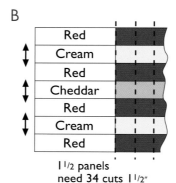

1 1/2 panels
need 34 cuts 1 1/2"

F

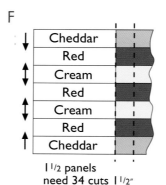

1 1/2 panels
need 34 cuts 1 1/2"

D

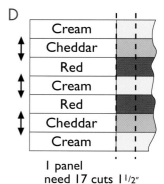

1 panel
need 17 cuts 1 1/2"

E

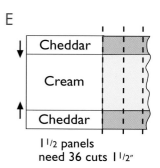

1 1/2 panels
need 36 cuts 1 1/2"

F

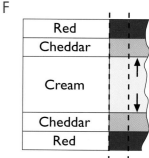

1 1/2 panels
need 36 cuts 1 1/2"

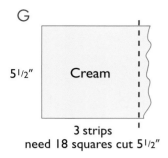

G

5¹/₂" Cream

3 strips
need 18 squares cut 5¹/₂"

Triple Irish Chain block assembly

Lay out strips in the order shown below.
Sew strips together. Make 17 blocks.

Alternate block assembly

Lay out strips in the order shown below.
Sew into three rows. Join the rows to make
the block. Press to cream square.
Make 18 blocks.

A B C D C B A

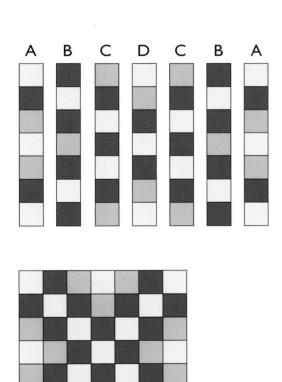

F

E

G

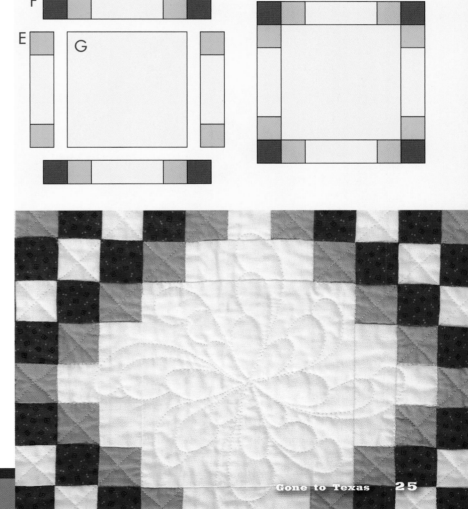

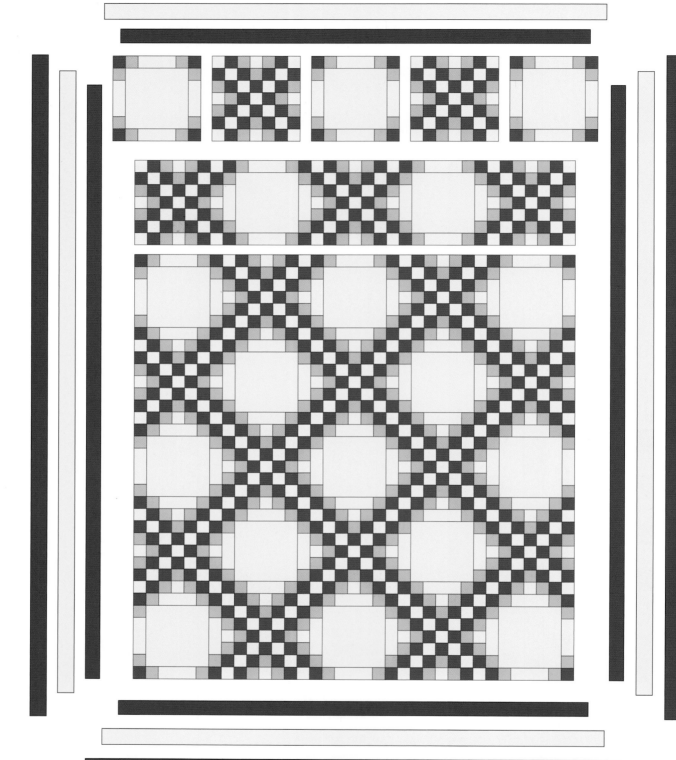

Quilt top assembly

Arrange blocks in to 7 rows of 5 blocks alternating a Triple Irish Chain block and an Alternate block as shown in the assembly diagram. Sew in rows. Join the rows together.

Borders

Add three borders; the first border is red, second border is cream and the third border is red. Add sides first, then top and bottom.

Measure your quilt top through the middle from top to bottom. Join lengths of the 2" red border strips to match your measurement. Sew to the sides of the quilt, pressing to the border.

Measure your quilt top again, through the middle from side to side. Join lengths of the 2" red border strips to match your measurement. Sew to the top and bottom of the quilt, pressing to the border.

Repeat the process with the inner cream border and the outer red border.

Finishing

Triple Irish Chain was machine quilted a grid in the pieced blocks and a feather design in the plain blocks. Bind with cheddar fabric to finish.

Soldiers Parade

Texas seceded from the Union in February 1861. The Civil War began in April that same year. The war years were extremely hard on the South economically and emotionally. Texas seemed to fare better than the rest of the South, especially in regards to livestock. Having dairy cows, meant butter for your family or to sell.

Farm wives had to sustain the farm and family in their husband's absence well as continuing to care for the family with their normal duties. Lizzie's journal entries reflect these hardships as Robert joined the army on July 5, 1862, and her agony over the war.

1861

June

11th scalded the beds   Sis came down and I helped her on her flag

12th worked on the flag

July

20th made Gippy a little coat and went to the muster in the eve   They are having dreadful times in Missouri and Virginia we here   Oh it is dreadful

September

21st Mr Carpenter went to McKinney to see the boys off for the wars – Stones regiment is encamped at McKinney

29th Mr Carpenter went up on white rock Col Parson's regiment is encamped

30th spun some in the morning Mrs Bush and I went up to see the soldiers encamped up on white rock- we saw them parade and exercise with the sword

October

1st sewed on the tent for the Bastrop Company Capt Hy Smith   Mary Ann helped me sew

2nd went over to Mas sewed on the tent   walked home and led my horse

3rd sewed on the tent and helped about dinner

4th finished the tent and a couple of soldiers came after it

29th John brought my sewing machine this evening or rather night

30th Annie came over to day worked some on my machine I like it very well so far went up to Mas in the eve

1862

February

27th dreary times don't feel much like work this day have just heard the feds have taken Bowlingreen Ky and Fort Dolison Tenn O that this dreadful war was at an end

28th Worked a little but don't remember at what but patched some in the morning We all feel very badly over the defeat of our armies   I hope they will never have another defeat

I fear we all will have a dreadful time before our Independence is declared-but with the help of providence we will succeed

continued on page 32

Soldiers Parade

1861
63" X 87"

MADE BY BETSY CHUTCHIAN
BLOCKS PIECED BY SONJA KRAUS
QUILTED BY SHERI MECOM

BLOCKS 9" FINISHED

Fabrics

4 1/2 yards of cream – 2 1/2 yards for wide border strips and alternate strips and 2 yards for top and bottom borders and block piecing.

1/3 yard each of 9 different prints of the same color family. This quilt was made with madder red, but indigo or turkey red would also be good choices.

2 yards extra-wide 108" muslin or 5 1/2 yards 44" wide fabric of choice for backing.

5/8 yard of brown or madder red for binding.

Cutting

From cream, cut:
2 ½ yards, cut again into 2 lengthwise strips 10½" wide (for borders) and 2 lengthwise strips 8 ½" wide (for alternate strips). Set aside.
2 yards, cut again into 2 lengthwise strips 4" wide. Set aside.

From remaining cream, cut:
41 – 4 ¼" squares, cut again from corner to corner diagonally twice.
81 – 3 1/8" squares.

From dark prints, cut:
54 – 5 3/8" squares, cut again from corner to corner diagonally once.
81 – 3 1/8" squares.

Block assembly

Make half-square triangle units from the cream and dark 3 1/8" squares. Draw a diagonal line on each cream square. With right sides together stitch on each side of the drawn line with a scant one-quarter-inch seam. Give each sewn square a quick press then cut apart on drawn line. Press each triangle unit to the dark fabric. Trim to 2 5/8" square. Make 162 half-square triangle units.

Lay out the units as shown below. Sew block as follows. Make 54 units.

Sew 2 units together to make one block. Make 27 blocks.

Quilt top assembly

Lay out blocks into 3 vertical strips of 9 blocks each. Sew together. Press to large triangles.

Measure each pieced strip. Strips should measure 81 1/2", but because of differences in seam allowances and pressing, your strips may measure longer or shorter. Join lengths of the 8 1/2" wide cream alternate strips to match the measurement of pieced strips. Referring to the assembly guide for placement and the note below, sew one pieced vertical strip alternating with one 8 1/2" cream strip. Press to the cream strip. Repeat until all three pieced strips are sewn to both alternating strips.

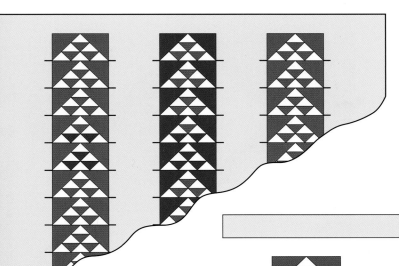

Note: In order for the pieced strips and alternate strips to line up correctly, it is important to take time to pin at the beginning and the end of the strips and evenly distributed points between. (half, quarter, etc. for the cream strips).

To achieve even distribution and a visually consistent horizontal line, mark match points as shown above on the wrong side of the cream after adding the first cream strip that will match the corresponding seam line on the next pieced strip. Use your ruler as a guide to mark the points. The wrong side of the quilt is shown.

1862 *continued*

June 30th

I believe this is the warmest day we have had this summer   we are hoping that it will drive all the Lincolns men from the south

July

5th Mr Carpenter went to McKinney and joined a company

25th Milla washed to day and I got dinner for the men that was thrashing they finished to day and I am glad made Ellen a slip and worked on Mr Carpenter a blanket

26th finished Mr Carpenters blanket and marked it and mended and marked his clothes and made him a pair of saddle pockets to carry his clothes for he is about to start for the wars

1863

January 12th

Finished Ann a dress and made me a white flannel skirt and fixed Jeffy a night gown Ben brought me a couple of letters from my dear husband and also a pair of cards

February 2nd

cut out my $30 cotton dress and made a skirt

March *(dates are lost)*

Went to Spring Creek to Meeting   subject was resurrection from the dead Mary Ann went in the buggy with me went by R Browns and broke our gear in the creek

Went up to Ma's and worked on Johnys shirt   My dear husband got back from the army to day

My dear husband is here and all's right

Expenses
Paid Mr Crozier for buggy 60.00
Paid Bro Carlton 42.00
Cabbage seed   .25

Paid Nichols 12.00
28 ½ yds cotton 42.75

April 23rd

went as far as Owens with my dear husband on his way to the army   this evening has been indeed a dull lonely evening

25th Went to look for a cow this morning a very hard storm in the evening

27th Finished Mr Carpenters overshirt and drove up some cows and young cows

Proffits Butter 7.00

Borders

Cut the 10 1/2" side borders to your measurement found above. Pin in the same manner as for the 8 1/2" cream strips, half, quarter, etc. to ensure the sides go on evenly. Sew the borders to each side.

Measure width of your quilt. Cut the reserved 4" strips to that measurement. Sew strips to top and bottom.

Finishing

The quilting closely replicates that done on the antique quilt. It features a gorgeous winding feather border with narrow clamshells and filled triangles are quilted on the outer borders with triple hanging diamonds filling the alternate strips. The pieced strips have two different overall designs diagonally crossing the triangles.

Bind with a brown or madder red fabric.

Gone to Texas

Gone to Texas is a fabric lover's quilt, a mosaic-like display of blocks and pieces that forces the viewer to look beyond the quilt design, and instead, study every individual fabric. I love scrap quilts and this example on page 15 holds one of the best collections of fabrics I have ever seen with scraps and larger pieces most likely taken from garment making. I can easily envision Lizzie having enough scraps to make a quilt like this.

Not only was Lizzie a prolific quiltmaker, but making clothes for herself, family, slaves, hired folks and others was an everyday matter of fact part of her life. Her scrap bag must have been filled with a multitude of various fabrics.

1860

April 18 Mr Carpenter is shearing sheep

1862

April 30th picking my black wool yet
John Brown is here making me a loom I guess I will have to pick in earnest now

25th sister came and helped me put in my peace for blankets I wove about a yard this evening my loom works fine

26th wove 4 yds the reaper here cutting oats Mary Ann came over in the evening to see how my new loom does

1863

January 17th Very cool yet to day
but the snow has melted considerable and it is very mudy Jim went to mill and Willy and I had to watch the sheep two pigs got out of the run and killed two lambs in short order we got them back knit some to day

19th finished me a chemise and raced around after the pigs and lambs through the mud which was shoe top deep a damp misty bad day

31st Put a belt in Jeffys lincy dress and patched some I believe I took a ride in the evening after the sheep took little Jeff with me drove home 16 and 4 lambs Not a very pretty day put a lock on my granary door to day

February 23rd I carded some and
made some garden the first of the season I was out in the evening driving up some sheep

24th Went this morning to hunt Jeffys shoe I lost it yesterday looking for the sheep Expenses 28 ½ yds cotton 42.75

1867

June 28th I made through the past
week a pair of pants myself a dress Mr Carpenter a pair of drawers and peaced on my quilt some--I have my rolls now and as I have a great deal of spinning to do I want to get at it in the morning

1869

Aug 8th This week I finished Willy a shirt
made Bobbie a white boddie and myself a dress -buff gingham-myself a bonnet – washed and ironed some little and made myself a riding skirt went to meeting Friday and Saturday

Work that I have done in 1869 besides my housework which consists of cooking washing ironing etc – peaced 3 old quilts and finished one new – cut and made number of articles 119 – spun yarn 50, knit socks 9 pair
Goods at Mr Pooles
Calico 9yds 1.50
spool thread 30cts
Green calico 6 yds 75 cts
Lawn dress 10cts per yd 80 cts
Cotton for chemise 50cts

continued on page 43

Gone to Texas

CIRCA 1860-1870
72" X 73 1/2"

MADE BY BETSY CHUTCHIAN
(THE UNION BLOCKS WERE PART OF A BLOCK
EXCHANGE WITH THE 19TH CENTURY PATCHWORK DIVAS.)
QUILTED BY SHERI MECOM

Fabrics

9-10 yards total of fabrics ranging in size from scraps to fat quarters to half-yard cuts.

Note: This quilt needs a large selection of browns, madder reds, rusty oranges, double pinks and soft muted purples. Also needed in smaller quantities are shirting fabrics, indigos and poison greens. Start with one-quarter yard pieces or fat quarters and search your scrap bag.

5 yards backing in fabric of your choice.

5/8 yard binding in fabric of your choice to match the top.

Cutting

Gone To Texas is made from a variety of pieced blocks: 17 Union blocks, 1 Odd block, 7 Delectable Union blocks, 6 Shoo-fly blocks in two sizes and 1 Sawtooth blocks. Numerous half-square triangles, squares, and rectangles are used as fillers to finish the quilt.

Because so many fabrics are used in each block, it is important to determine which fabrics you want to use for each block as you make the blocks. Refer to the photo of the quilt for ideas in values and placement.

Union block

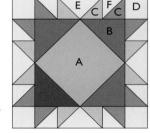

10 1/2" finished
Make 24 blocks. Note: 7 blocks will be reserved to make the Delectable Union blocks.

Cutting for one Union block
Determine which fabrics you want to use and cut:
1 – 5 1/2" square (A).
2 – 4 1/2" squares, cut again diagonally once (B).
8 – 2 5/8" squares, cut again diagonally once (C).

Cutting cont.

4 – 2 1/4" squares (D).
1 – 4 3/4" square, cut again diagonally twice (E).
4 – 2 5/8" squares, cut again diagonally once (F).

Union block assembly

Referring to the block diagram above, lay out all pieces.
Then sew as follows:

 Trim to 7 1/2."

 Make 4.

 Make 8.

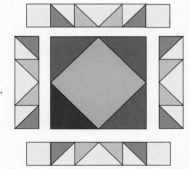

Make
24 blocks.

Odd block

10 1/2" finished
Make 1 block.
Note: The odd block is the center of one of the Delectable Union blocks. Finishing instructions are to the right in the Delectable Union instructions.

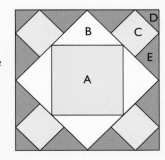

Cutting for one Odd block

Determine which fabrics you want to use and cut:
1 – 5 3/4" square (A).
2 – 4 5/8" squares, cut again diagonally once (B).
4 – 3" squares (C).
2 – 2 5/8" squares, cut again diagonally once (D).
2 – 4 3/4" squares, cut again diagonally twice (E).

Odd block assembly

Referring to the block diagram, lay out all pieces.
Then sew as follows:
Make 1 block.

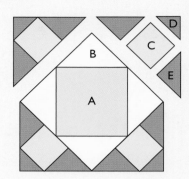

Delectable Union

15" finished
Use 7 **Union blocks** and 1 **Odd block** as centers for the block

Corner assembly

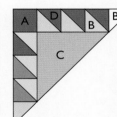

Remember these are very scrappy blocks.
Make 32.

Cutting for one corner unit

Determine which fabrics you want to use and cut:
1 – 2" square (A).
4 – 2 3/8" squares, cut again diagonally once (B).
1 – 5 3/8" square, cut again diagonally once (C).
Note: Reserve the spare triangle for use in another corner unit.
3 – 2 3/8" squares, cut again diagonally twice (D).

Shoo-Fly block

7 1/2" finished
Make 5.

6" finished
Make 1.

**Cutting for one 7 1/2"
Shoo-Fly block**

Determine which fabrics you want to use and cut:

1 – 3" square (A).

2 – 3 3/8" squares, cut again diagonally once (B).

2 – 3 3/8" squares, cut again diagonally once (C).

4 – 3" squares (D).

**Cutting for one 6"
Shoo-Fly block**

Determine which fabrics you want to use and cut:

1 – 2 1/2" square (A).

2 – 2 7/8" squares, cut again diagonally once (B).

2 – 2 7/8" squares, cut again diagonally once (C).

4 – 2 1/2" squares (D).

Lay out the elements for one corner unit as shown. Make 6 half-square triangle units from triangles D and B. Press to the dark. Stitch three of these half-square triangle units and one triangle B together. Sew this to the large triangle C. Stitch the remaining half-square triangles together with a square A on one end and the remaining triangle B on the together, referring to the diagram for placement. Stitch the two units together. Make 4 per block.

Delectable Union block

To finish the Delectable Union blocks, add 4 pieced corners to each of the reserved Union blocks and Odd block. Referring to the diagram, lay out all the block units and sew.

Shoo-Fly block assembly

Sew 4 half-square triangle units from triangles B and C. Referring to the diagram, lay out all the pieces and sew into rows. Press to the plain squares D. Join rows.

Sawtooth block

7 1/2" finished
Make 4.

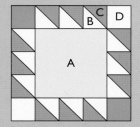

Cutting for one Sawtooth block

Determine which fabrics you want to use and cut:

1 – 5" square (A).

6 – 2 3/8" squares, cut again diagonally once (B).

6 – 2 3/8" squares, cut again diagonally once (C).

4 – 2" squares (D).

Sawtooth block assembly

Sew 12 half-square triangle units from triangles B and C. Trim to 2". Referring to the diagram, lay out all the pieces and sew into rows. Press to the plain squares D on the top and bottom rows and press to the large square A on the center row. Join the rows. Press rows in one direction.

Quilt section assembly

Many half-square triangle units, squares and rectangles complete the quilt. Once you have assembled the blocks you may begin sewing sections together, adding the filler pieces. Refer to quilt photo for color placements.

Section 1

Elements for Section 1 include: 5 Shoo-Fly blocks, 3 Sawtooth blocks, 28 small and 1 medium half-square triangle units, 3 small squares and 2 rectangles. Once the following filler units are made, refer to the assembly diagram on page 42 and assembly Section 1.

refer to the assembly diagram on page 42

Small half-square triangle units

1 1/2" finished
Make 28.

Cut 14 – 2 3/8" light squares, cut again diagonally once.
Cut 14 – 2 3/8" dark squares, cut again diagonally once.
Sew triangles together and press to the dark.

Medium half-square triangle unit

3" finished
Make 1.

Cut 1 – 3 7/8" light square, cut again diagonally once.

Cut 1 – 3 7/8" dark square, cut again diagonally once. Sew triangles together and press to the dark. *Note*: There will be one half-square triangle unit leftover. You can use this in another section.

Squares

Cut 4 – 2" squares.

Rectangles

Cut 2 – 2" x 3 1/2" rectangles.

Section 2

Elements for Section 2 include: 5 Union blocks, 1 small Shoo-Fly block, 1 Sawtooth block, 55 small and 2 medium half-square triangle units, 40 small and 1 large squares and 1 rectangle. Once the following filler units are made, refer to the assembly diagram and assembly Section 2.

Small half-square triangle units

1 1/2" finished
Make 55.

Cut 1 light and 1 dark square. Refer to Section 1 for cutting and piecing instructions. *Note:* There will be one half-square triangle unit leftover. You can use this in another section.

Medium half-square triangle units

3" finished
Make 2.

Cut 1 light and 1 dark square. Refer to Section 1 for cutting and piecing instructions.

Squares

Cut 40 – 2" squares.

Cut 1 – 3 1/2" square.

Rectangle

Cut 1 – 2" x 3 1/2" rectangle.

Tip: Assemble 15 – four-patch units using 30 – 1 1/2" triangle units and 30 squares for the left side of Section 2, then finish filling in the section.

Section 3

Elements for Section 3 include: 8 Delectable Union blocks; 1 of those has the Odd block in the center; 6 small and 5 medium half-square triangle units; 6 small, 3 medium and 2 large squares; and 2 rectangles. Once the following filler units are made, refer to the assembly diagram and assembly Section 3.

Small half-square triangle units

1 1/2" finished
Make 6.

Cut 3 light and 3 dark squares. Refer to Section 1 for piecing instructions.

Medium half-square triangle units

3" finished
Make 5.

Cut 3 light and 3 dark squares. Refer to Section 1 for piecing instructions.
Note: There will be one half-square triangle unit leftover. You can use this in another section

Squares

Cut 6 – 2" squares.

Cut 3- 3 1/2" squares.

Cut 2 – 6 1/2" squares.

Rectangles

Cut 2 – 2" x 3 1/2" rectangles.

Assemble 4 – four-patch units as in Section 2, then finish filling in the section.

Section 4

Elements for Section 4 include: 12 Union blocks; 2 small and 10 medium half-square triangle units; and 10 small squares. Once the following filler units are made, refer to the assembly diagram in assembly Section 4.

Small half-square triangle units

1 1/2" finished
Make 10.

Cut 5 light and 5 dark squares. Refer to Section 1 for piecing instructions.

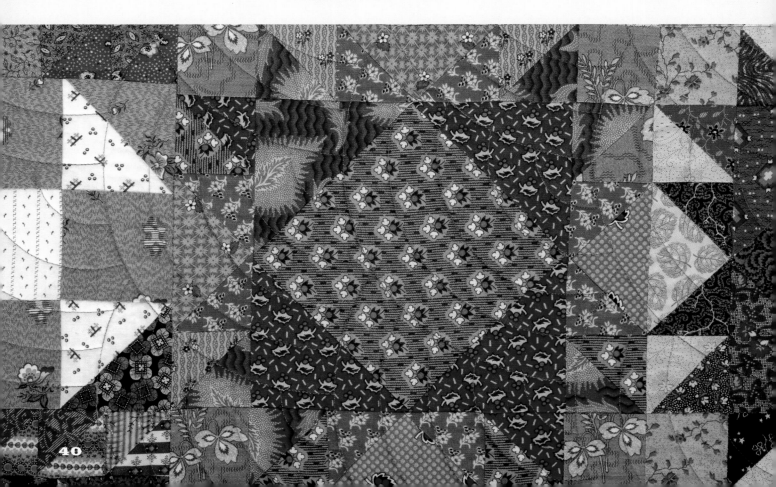

Medium half-square triangle units

3" finished
Make 2.

Cut 1 light and 1 dark squares. Refer to Section 1 for piecing instructions.

Squares

Cut 10 – 2" squares.

Section 5

Elements for Section 5 include: 80 small, 5 medium and 3 large half-square triangle units; 62 squares; and a total of 20 rectangles in various sizes. Once the following filler units are made, refer to the assembly diagram and assembly Section 5.

Small half-square triangle units

1 1/2" finished
Make 80.

Cut 40 light and 40 dark squares. Refer to Section 1 for piecing instructions.

Medium half-square triangle units

2 1/4" finished
Make 5.

Cut 3 – 3 1/8" light squares, cut again diagonally once.

Cut 3 – 3 1/8" dark squares, cut again diagonally once.

Sew triangles together and press to the dark.
Note: There will be one half-square triangle unit leftover. You can use this in another section.

Large half-square triangle units

3" finished
Make 3.

Cut 2 light and 2 dark squares. Refer to Section 1 for piecing instructions.
Note: There will be one half-square triangle unit leftover. You can use this in another section.

Small squares

Cut 62 – 2" squares.

Rectangles

Cut 2 – 1 5/8" x 2 ¾" rectangles.
Cut 7 – 2" x 5" rectangles.
Cut 2 – 2 3/4" x 5" rectangles.
Cut 9 – 2" x 3 1/2" rectangles.

Tip: Make 22 – four-patch units in contrasting fabrics as shown in Section 2, then proceed to fill in the section.

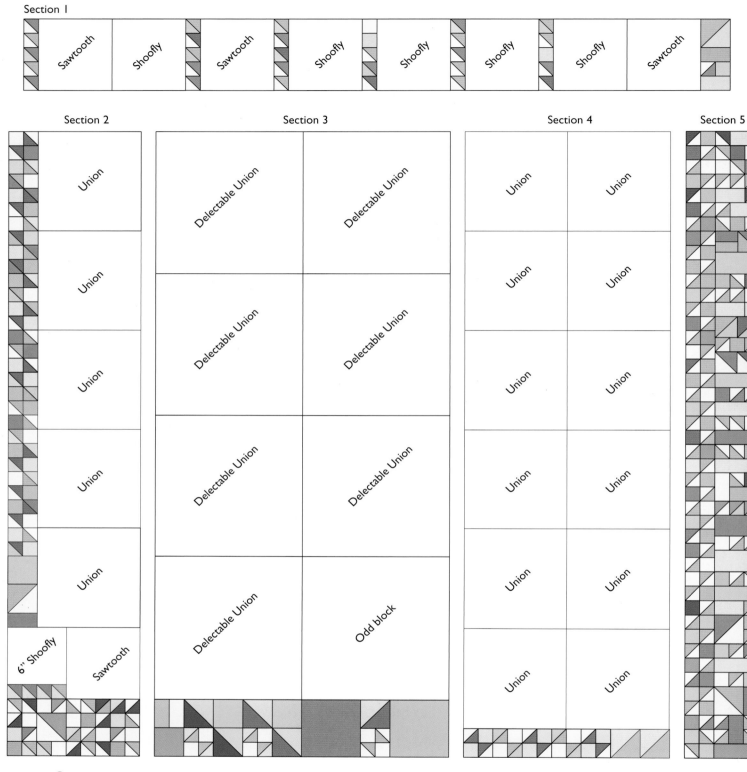

Section 1

| | Sawtooth | Shoofly | | Sawtooth | | Shoofly | | Shoofly | | Shoofly | | Shoofly | Sawtooth | |

Section 2 — Union, Union, Union, Union, Union, 6" Shoofly, Sawtooth

Section 3 — Delectable Union, Delectable Union, Delectable Union, Delectable Union, Delectable Union, Delectable Union, Delectable Union, Odd block

Section 4 — Union, Union, Union, Union, Union

Section 5

Quilt top assembly

Referring to the quilt photo and the assembly diagram, sew sections 2, 3, 4 and 5 together. Add section 1 to the top, last.

Finishing

Gone To Texas was quilted with the Baptist Fan pattern. Bind in a fabric of your choice.

continued from page 34

1870

January 11th last week
I finished and bound a new quilt that some of my
kind neighbors helped me to quilt

February 18th This week our little boys
four of them have been laid up with the measles   I
have no work to report for this week except my
housework and wait on the sick

April 27th Yesterday I went to Plano – some
of Mr Oglesby's new goods have come, the store
was crowded on yesterday – Last week I put in and
quilted a quilt for the little bed

May 1st this past week I put in a comfort and
quilted it

December 18th Tis is the anniversary
of our Wedding – 19 years ago to day we were joined
in holy wedlock- away back in Our Old Ky. Home 19
years have passed in almost unbroken happiness
since that day by our humbled selves...My mind
runs back to that evening- so long ago- and it seems
almost but yesterday – so vivid is the picture. It was
all cold and snowy without- but warm and pleasant
within and eyes full of love and cheeks of health and
lips of sweetness and words of gaiety and where to
day they are gone, some one way and some another,
some are long since in there graves and some are
scattered

31st During the past year 1870 I have made 126
garments quilted quilts 2 peaced and quilted one
comfort – spun cuts of yarn 13-knit gloves and socks
and stockings 9 or 10 pair – done my cooking and
Ironing and cleaning and scouring and a good many
other things

Gathering Baskets

Recorded throughout the journals are references to gathering vegetables from the garden or plums, pecans, dewberries, persimmons and grapes that grew wild on their property. On March 14, 1863, Lizzie wrote, "Anna and sister, myself and Kate Mathews and some of the little boys all went grape hunting down at the Alston place – got no grapes but got some dewberries."

In 1872, Lizzie mentions making a basket quilt by name. When I read this, I immediately thought of her carrying a basket when she and the boys went out gathering. Was her basket quilt a tribute to such a normal everyday task? Or perhaps, did she just enjoy the pattern?

1871

September 9th The boys have picked our little patch of cotton once and have been gathering some corn, have 22 loads in the crib which I guess will make near 300 bushels. I have all my sewing done that is needful just now. I recon I can work on some quilts

October 4th The past week I made Willy a shirt and Bennie a boddie and knit a goodeal- peaced some on my quilt basket

November 12th I have been doing my house work as Mary the girl I hired had got tired and quit and now I have so much to do I hardly know what to do first – my winters sewing and the babe to attend to in addition to my house work

December 10th To day is Ma's birthday She is 70 years old to day – Time flies

Work for 1871

I made 115 garments – knit 12 pairs of socks and stockings – peaced and quilted 3 quilts-cut carpet rags for 20 yards of carpet – done my house work four months of the year - besides sickness

1872

April 7th I worked on my basket quilt some and patched some such bad weather I did not do very much of anything

14th Mr Carpenter and myself and Willy went to meeting to day Bro P Smith preached there was only a few out – as the day was unfavorable I left the baby with johny and went horse back – Bro Bagby came home with us to dinner I have done little settled work went to help Mrs Bush on her basket quilt ma went with me – peaced on my basket quilt

29th Mr C myself and some of the boys went to Bro Clint Haggards to a quilting – good many persons there – to day Mr Lyle is here altering colts – goodby frolicksome April Made a little sac and peaced an old quilt

December 10th This is rather a wintry looking day, last night it hailed a little round hail and this morning it has turned to snow is snowing now in Old Kentucky style - which finds fair to soon make it pretty good Sleighing- All as well as common now except myself I have a very sore breast and it has been sore for nearly a week it is very much swollen and pains me very badly I think it will have to be opened soon- to day is Ma's birthday she is 71 years old to day- My chickens have died up with the chicken cholera so I have no eggs at all to make her a cake - Ma's have also died and her turkeys also- The children keep up a mighty noise and carry in a heap of snow

Gathering Baskets

1871
49 1/2" X 58 7/8"

MADE BY BETSY CHUTCHIAN
QUILTED BY SHERI MECOM

BLOCKS 6 1/4" FINISHED

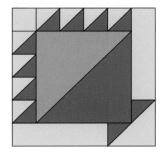

Fabrics

2 yards pink for background and borders.

3/4 yard total assorted indigo prints.

3/8 yard total assorted medium brown prints in small amounts: scraps, fat quarters or fat eighths.

2 1/4 yards poison green for setting blocks, borders and binding.

3 3/4 yards for backing.

Cutting

From pink, cut:
8 – 2 1/2" strips x length of fabric. Reserve for borders.
Reserve the rest of the pink for blocks.

From poison green cut:
4 squares 10 1/8" for setting triangles, cut again diagonally twice.

12 squares 6 3/4" for setting squares.

2 – 5 3/8" squares for corners.

5 to 6 – 3 1/4" wide strips by width of fabric, for middle border.

6 – 2 1/4" strips for binding.

For 20 blocks cut:
From reserved pink, cut:
20 – 1 1/2" squares.
80 – 2" squares.
10 – 3 3/8" squares, cut again diagonally once.
40 – 1 3/4" x 4 1/4" rectangles.

From assorted indigo fabrics, cut:
80 – 2" squares.
10 – 4 7/8" squares.
20 – 2 1/8" squares, cut again diagonally once.

From assorted medium brown prints, cut:
10 – 4 7/8" squares.

Block assembly

Make 20.

Make half square triangles from 80 – 2" squares of pink and 80 of indigo. Draw a diagonal line on the back side of the pink squares. Match up a pink and an indigo square. With right sides together, stitch a scant one-quarter inch on each side of drawn line as shown.

Cut apart on drawn line.
Press seams open.

Trim units to 1 1/2". This will yield 160 half-square triangles. Use 8 of them for 1 block.

Lay out all the elements for one block shown in the diagram below. Mix and match the indigo fabrics with different browns for a scrappy look. Stitch block together as follows. Press following arrows on diagram.

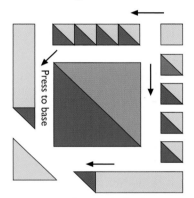

Press to basket base

Press to large triangle unit

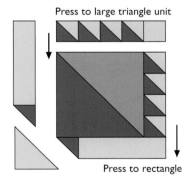

Press to rectangle

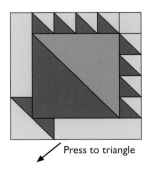

Press to triangle

Quilt top assembly

Lay out the basket blocks, squares, setting triangles and corners in diagonal rows as shown in the assembly diagram. Stitch rows together. Press to setting pieces.

Borders

Add three borders; the first border is pink, middle border is green and the outer border is pink. Add sides first, then top and bottom.

Measure your quilt top through the center from top to bottom. Cut 2 lengths of the reserved 2 1/2" pink border strips to match your measurement. Sew to the sides of the quilt, pressing to the border.

Measure your quilt top again, through the center from side to side. Cut lengths of the reserved 2 1/2" pink border strips to match your measurement. Sew to the top and bottom of the quilt, pressing to the border.

Repeat the process to add the 3 1/4" wide inner green border and then the 2 1/2" wide pink outer border.

Finishing

Gathering Baskets is quilted in a cross hatch grid in the body of the quilt and a cable design across the borders.

Bind in poison green fabric.

Half Star

Lizzie mentioned so few of her quilt patterns by name that when she did, I took particular note. When I read about **Lizzie's Half Star** quilt, I could not stop thinking about what that pattern might look like. Since I had never heard of it, I researched it in several of my quilt pattern reference books. I couldn't find anything by that name.

Then I saw antique quilt of the same era owned by my friend, Connie Watkins, shown left, and I realized what the pattern was – two Lemoyne Stars split in half set in a square design – the **Half Star Quilt!**

1873

February 26th Made Jeffy a shirt and quilted some and would have got out my quilt but was not at all well-very severe cold I think

March 23rd The week that has passed I went visiting twice...made a shirt for Bobbie   commenced a quilt, the half star

March 31st The past week I made Mr C a pair of drawers and a pair of slips for pillows and a couple of bolster slips and patched some....I peaced some on my quilt -4 half star

April 13th The past week I finished peacing my half star quilt - I also made two garments and went visiting one day and went to Plano one day

June 23rd My hired help have gone and I am chief cook and the workmen have hardly make a beginning on the house

July 1st This is a tolerably pleasant day- high wind – some prospect for rain I think- we are by no means prepared for it just now as the workmen have the roof off the house and everything tore up terrible – heap

continued on page 53

Half Star Quilt

1873
56" X 72"

MADE AND QUILTED BY BETSY CHUTCHIAN.

BLOCKS 8" FINISHED

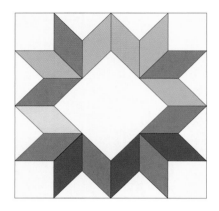

Fabrics

1 1/2 yards shirting.

1 yard or more total assorted madder reds, purples, browns and other fabrics as desired.

3 3/4 yards poison green – 1 3/4 yards for setting and first border, 2 yards for outer border.

5/8 yard madder red for middle border.

5/8 yard madder red or green for binding.

5 yards backing.

Cutting

From assorted dark prints, cut:
288 diamonds from 1 5/8" strips, cut at a 45° angle and then cut at 1 5/8" intervals, measuring parallel to first diagonal cut.

From shirting fabric, cut:
36 – 3 5/8" squares, cut again from corner to corner on both diagonals to yield 144 triangles.

72 – 2 1/8" squares for corners
18 – 3 7/8" squares for block centers

From poison green (1 5/8 yard piece), cut:
2 lengthwise strips 2 1/2" wide for top and bottom of first border.
17 - 8 1/2" squares.

From poison green (2 yard piece), cut:
2 lengthwise strips 2 1/2" wide for sides of first border.
4 lengthwise strips 4 1/2" wide for the outer border.

From madder red, cut:
7 – 2 1/2" strips by width of fabric for middle border.

Block assembly

Select 16 diamonds per block, 8 triangles and 4 small squares per block. Mark one-quarter inch seam points on all pieces as shown in diagram below. Measure one-quarter inch from the outside edges to mark dots.

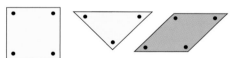

Stitch diamonds together in pairs without crossing seams. Pin and carefully stitch between seam dots, backstitching at the beginning and end, starting and stopping on the dots. Stitch 2 pairs of diamonds together (1). For each block, make 4 sets of 4 diamonds. Press consistently in one direction (2).

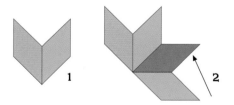

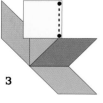
Stitch corner to diamond unit from outside in toward center (3). Matching dots, backstitch at the beginning and end, starting and stopping on the dots. Keep the seams free, pinning as needed.
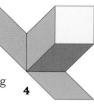

Flip square to the other side and repeat stitching process from outside in toward center (4).

Add triangles to diamonds with the same stitching process matching dots, backstitching at beginning and end, starting and stopping on the dots. Sew from the outside in toward the middle, pinning seams out of the way as needed. Flip triangle to other side of diamond and repeat process. Press all seams in the same direction (5).

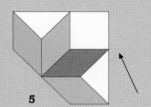

5

Make 4 half stars per block.
Join four half stars to center square. Mark seam dots on each square as shown. Match dots on square to diamond dots. Stitch between dots, backstitching at the beginning and end, starting and stopping on the dots. Press to center square. Repeat on the opposite two sides.

Fold block in half. Stitch diamonds between seam dots as shown

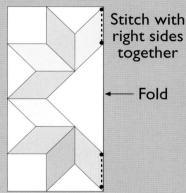

Stitch with right sides together

← **Fold**

Fold again and repeat on other side.
Make 18 blocks.

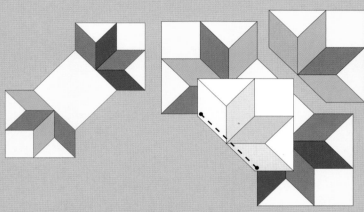

1873 *continued*

of work to do and don't know where to get any help – I have not been well for several days – I have no appetite to eat and sick at the stomach most of the time This past week I have done nothing but cook and Iron and patch sweep make beds etc – no help but the little boys – and work hands here

October 7th some of the boys have gone pecan hunting to day

16th Sunday was my birth day – 41 years old – oh how good the Lord has been to me – to allow me to live so long so little ill ....Tennessee has suffered this year in that respect – at Nashville the cholera and at Memphis the yellow fever – the people of Shreveport La are in great distress with yellow fever at this time

November 2nd Mr C and the boys have been hauling cotton to the gin – Mr C bought me a sewing machine the past week – a Wheeler and Wilson $85- an old machine

Quilt top assembly

Lay out blocks into 7 rows of 5 blocks alternating a pieced block with a green 8 1/2" setting square. Sew blocks together as shown in the assembly diagram. Press seams to setting squares. Join rows together. Press rows all in one direction.

Borders

Add three borders; the first border is green, middle border is red and the outer border is green. Add sides first, then top and bottom.

Measure your quilt top through the middle from top to bottom. If necessary, join lengths of the 2 1/2" green border strips to match the measurement. Sew to the sides of the quilt, pressing to the border.

Measure your quilt top again, through the middle from side to side. Join lengths of the 2 1/2" green border strips to match the measurement. Sew to the top and bottom of the quilt, pressing to the border.

Repeat the process with the 2 1/2" strips for the middle red border and the 4 1/2" strips for the outer green border.

Finishing

Half Star Quilt is quilted in a diagonal grid across the alternate blocks. Across the pieced blocks, the quilting lines make an X that continues the grid then in the ditch around the diamonds.

Bind with madder red or green.

Lizzie's Plated Hexagon

The charm of the Hexagon seems to be endless for quilters. Lizzie made at least four hexagon quilts that she mentioned by name. Was it because it took small amounts of leftover scraps? She would have had quite a stash of scraps from her garment making as well as her other household sewing. Templates would have been scraps of newspapers cut into hexagon shapes – also easy for her to come by.

I imagined the plates that Lizzie mentioned to be the circular "plates" of color with a path surrounding each one. If Lizzie had made a quilt using a black fabric for the path, it would most likely have been black wool or silk. She made at least two like this, the Plated Hexagon in 1869 and the other in 1880 for my great grandfather, Jefferson Davis Carpenter.

1861

January 4th got out my quilt and not sorry about either

25th   cut some quilt peaces and basted them

February 22nd   put in my hexicon quilt and quilted some – sister came to help me

26th got out my quilt and bound it   made some garden

April 15th peaced some on my quilt Grandma (Grandma Martin was a midwife) and I set in to picking wool

17th Sick   Jeffy born last night
(Betsy's great grandfather)

1869

February 28th   This week I only made Bobbie and myself an apron and peaced some on my hexigon quilt – I want to get it done this spring

March 18th   I finished up my hexigon quilt and have been quilting it – I get along slow- but will get done after a while Ma has helped me two days and talks of comeing to help me again – Mary Lunsford and Mary Mathews and Aronia has helped me

April 4th   I got out my quilt and bound it.

1874

March 24th   Very pretty day – Mary Ann came and spent the day with me. Martha washed and I was cook today – worked on my quilt this evening called the plated Hexicon.

28th   today was cool and cloudy. I went to Mrs. Bushes today, took Ma with me. Mrs. Bush had a little quilting – we had a nice time – got out the quilt and had some nice piano music

30th   A very damp foggy morning continued so until about 12 o'clock-cleared up. I worked on my plated Hexicon quilt – finishing it excepting some borders

June 17th   Ma came down this morning and we quilted on my plated hexicon quilt – it has been in a good while and now out yet. I was very thankful for the help. Tolerably warm day. All well thank God.

1880

February 3rd   Don't think I ever saw such a pretty snow – soft, so white - 12 to 14 inches deep – I cut some quilt peaces and sent them to ma while ago – she is peacing a quilt for me I want to give to Jeff - I must close now and get some work done

February 16th   As this is such a windy day I must note it down – it blows harder than common to day indeed – it seems like blowing all light substance clear away and a person can neither ride or walk with any kind of comfort – setting a quilt together to day – the plated hexigon Intended for J. D. Carpenter

Lizzie's Plated Hexagon

1861, 1868, 1874, 1880
66" X 82"

MADE AND QUILTED BY BETSY CHUTCHIAN

BLOCKS 1 1/2" FINISHED

Hexagon Template and Half-Hexagon Template.

Note: Hexagons are measured by the length of one of its sides, not the measurement across the hexagon.

Fabrics

35-39 fat quarters (approximately 9 yards) assorted fabrics in colors of your choice.

5 yards black fabric for path.

¾ yard black fabric for binding.

5 yards backing.

Additional supplies

1 1/2" hexagon and 1 1/2" Trapezoid (half hexagon) precut paper templates* OR cut your own paper templates from card stock (lighter weight than poster board) using the templates.
Paper clips
Sharp scissors
Needles for English Paper piecing and basting.
50 weight thread in matching colors or a color that blends well, like a soft brown shade.
Chalk pencil
Long ruler

Cutting

From the assorted colors for the 24 Plate blocks and 8 Half Plate blocks, cut:

39 – 4" square for center
218 – 4" squares for middle rings (contrasting fabric)
428 – 4" squares for outer rings (same as center fabric)

Note: 4" is a generous cut for the hexagons. If you are a more frugal quilter, you can cut them 3 1/2".

From the black, cut:

322 - 4" squares for the path hexagons.
32 – 2" x 4" rectangles for the half hexagons.

I recommend Paper Pieces brand packaged precut paper shapes, size 1 1/2". Ask for these at your local quilt shop or go to www.paperpieces.com to order them.

Preparing the hexagons

Place one paper template on the backside of one square of fabric. Pin in place, with a straight pin, centered. With sharp scissors, trim the fabric to the shape of the hexagon allowing a good quarter-inch seam all the way around. Fold one seam over the template and secure with a small paper clip. You may now remove the pin. The paper clip will hold the hexagon template and fabric together.

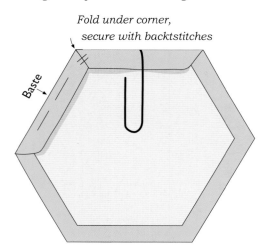

Fold under corner,
secure with backtstitches

Baste

Begin your basting stitch on a side to the right or left of the paper clip. Fold under one corner and secure with several stitches, just through the fabric. Take long stitches along the side of the hexagon through the fabric only until you reach the next corner. Fold the corner under and secure with several stitches then resume the long "traveling" stitches. Remove the paper clip when you approach the corner before the clip. Finish at the corner where you began with a couple of back stitches.

Plate block assembly

Make 24.
Each plate contains 1 center hexagon, 6 hexagons in middle and 12 on the outside. The outside hexagons and the center hexagon will be the same fabric, the middle hexagons will be the contrasting fabric. Refer to the drawings to create a total of 15 basted hexagons per Plate.

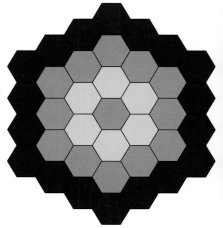

To join the hexagons to each other, take two prepared hexagon shapes starting with the center hexagon and one for the middle ring, stitch edges together as shown, right sides together with a tiny whipstitch in matching thread or thread that blends well.

Keep adding hexagons to the center until you have attached 6. Remove the center paper template now that it is enclosed. Fold the center in half, right sides together so that you may sew the sides of the hexagons. When all 6 are stitched in place, start to add the outer ring, one at a time until you have enclosed the middle ring. At this time remove the paper templates from the middle ring. With right sides, stitch the sides of the hexagons together, until all sides have been stitched to complete the Plate. You may reuse the templates when possible.

Half Plate block assembly

Make 8.
Each Half Plate contains 1 center hexagon, 4 hexagons in middle and 7 on the outside. The outside hexagons and the center hexagon will be the same fabric, the middle hexagons will be the contrasting fabric. Follow same instructions as above.

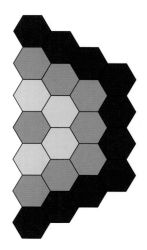

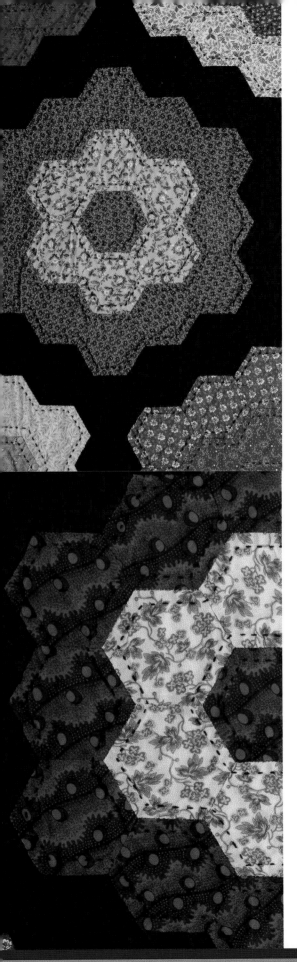

Background (Path) assembly and quilt assembly

Baste 322 black hexagons and 32 half hexagons.

Follow quilt diagram to add the black hexagons to the finished plates. This is a gradual process and you may wish to lay out your plates in a pleasing arrangement then note that arrangement on paper or take a snap shot of it for reference as you work row to row. At the top and bottom there are a few extra black hexagons that are added to complete the path as well as the half hexagons. This is illustrated with the white outline on the diagram. Note the position of the half plates on the diagram. As plates are enclosed by the path, you may remove the paper templates.

Finishing

Once all hexagons are stitched together and papers are removed, prepare the quilt for quilting in the manner of your choice. Lizzie's Plated Hexagon is hand quilted with black perle cotton in a utility, big stitch, style following the rings of each hexagon block and the path one quarter inch from the seams.

To eliminate the need to bind around every hexagon, square up the quilt. After quilting, stitch long basting stitches along both long sides of the quilt. After quilting, draw a line with a chalk pencil and ruler along both sides of the quilt where the pointed edges of the hexagons will be cut off.
Note: Do not cut away the points until after binding.

The guide for drawing and cutting will be the "v" parts of the hexagon. Refer to the assembly diagram and photo of the quilt to see where your line should be.

It is helpful to stitch the black binding on before you trim. To do this, line your binding even with the drawn line and sew. Trim points away flush with the binding. Sew binding down as usual.

Crowfoot

As I was researching the Crowfoot pattern that Lizzie mentioned in 1874, I found the same pattern carries different names – not an uncommon occurrence as names changed across the country. What I was delighted to realize is that I already knew this pattern very well. Several years ago, my sewing group made birthday blocks for me called Devil's Claw. An alternate name for Devil's Claw happens to be Crowfoot. So, my birthday block quilt quickly got a name change!

1874

February 23rd We had a pretty cold night last night. Ice this morning nearly an inch thick – did not melt today in the shade though the sun shines bright and cheerful. I worked on my quilt – Crowfoot – setting it together finished it except setting on some borders. The boys have been sowing oats today. Mr. Sage at work on the portico.

24th Tolerbly pretty day – somewhat cool. Mr. Carpenter went to McKinney. A gentleman came to see him to buy some mules. He remained all night. Martha washed, I cooked dinner and set some borders on my quilt.

March 11th Tolerbly cool day cloudy and rather disagreeable – I finished my carpet warp and reeled some – so cool they did not plant corn today. Mr. C made some picture frames and Willy and Gippy went to the bottom for wood.

13th cleaned the bedsteads and helped Martha scour in the morning. Made Eddie an apron in the evening. Clouded up and rained this evening. Mr Sage finished up everything and made a table for the school house today. He is done now. Some men out here to get a beef. I think the pararie beef poor now.

March 14th this is a gloomy morning - misting rain and tolerably cool – Mr. Leer is hanging the oil curtains in the new room...the children are nocking around some in one mischief and some another – noisy and troublesome. I am not very well, have a headache – which annoys my patching a little today, sweeping, etc., etc.

April 30th Mr Leer is making me some quilting frames

1876

March 9th Thursday I want to quilt some and try and get out the quilt that has been since Christmas

11th Saturday I finished quilting the crowfoot quilt to day and mended some

July 4th This morning I cleaned up the house above the stairs and below mended some half dozen garments - some five or six girls here today, or this evening to play Croquet - had a high time I recon - at least they all seemed very fond of the sport.

Crowfoot

1874-1876
76" X 76"

MADE BY BETSY CHUTCHIAN
QUILTED BY SHERI MECOM

BLOCKS 12" FINISHED

Fabric

2 yards total assorted light prints for blocks.

2 yards total assorted dark prints for blocks.

1 7/8 yards indigo for setting squares.

2 1/4 yards assorted indigos for borders.

5 yards for backing in fabric of your choice

5/8 yard for binding in fabric of your choice to match top.

Cutting

From assorted lights, cut:
48 – 2" squares.
48 – 3 1/2" squares.
144 – 2" x 3 1/2" rectangles.

From assorted darks, cut:
60 – 3 1/2" squares.
384 – 2" squares.

From indigo, cut:
13 – 12 1/2" squares for setting squares.

From assorted indigos, cut:
4 – 8 1/2" strips cut lengthwise. Reserve for border.

Crowfoot block assembly

To make 1 block
Each block is made of 8 Star-Point units, 4 Square-in-a-Square units, 5 large dark squares, 4 light rectangles and 4 light small squares.

Star-Point units

1 1/2" x 3" finished
Make 8.

Draw a diagonal line on the back side of 32 – 2" dark squares. This will be the stitching line when making star points and square in a square units.

Use 8 light rectangles and 16 – 2" dark squares to make the Star-Point units.

Match up one dark square on one light rectangle right sides together as shown. Stitch on drawn line.

Trim away excess fabric.

Press to corner.
Repeat on other side.

Square-in-a-Square units

3" finished
Make 4

Use 4 – 3 1/2" light squares and 16 – 2" dark squares to make the square-in-a-square units.
Position 1 dark square in each corner of 1 light square. Stitch on the drawn line. Trim away excess.

Press to corner.

Repeat on other three corners.

Block assembly

Referring to the block diagram, lay out the pieced for one block.
Stitch units together in rows.
Press to non-pieced squares and rectangles.

Stitch rows together, staggering seams. Make 12.

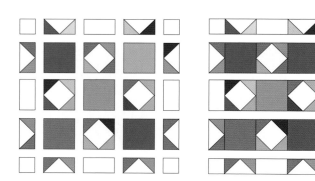

Quilt top assembly

Arrange blocks into 5 rows of 5 blocks alternating a Crowfoot block and a setting square as shown in the assembly diagram. Sew into rows, pressing to the setting squares. Join the rows together, pressing in one direction.

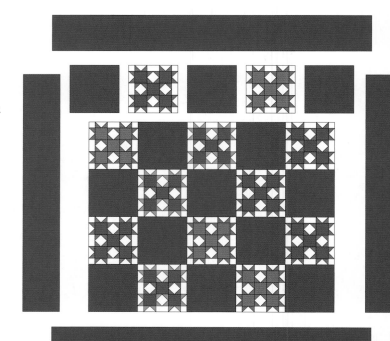

Borders

Measure your quilt top through the middle from top to bottom. Join 2 lengths of 8 1/4" wide assorted indigo border strips to match your measurement. Sew to the sides of the quilt, pressing to the border.

Measure your quilt top again, through the middle from side to side. Join 2 lengths of the border strips to match your measurement. Sew to the top and bottom of the quilt, pressing to the border.

Finishing

Crowfoot is quilted with a feathered wreath in the alternate blocks and an allover design in the pieced blocks.

Bind in fabric to match the quilt top.

Pieced Brickwork

Lizzie's habit of working on more than one quilt at a time was quite common but especially notable in 1876. She began **Crowfoot** in 1874 and completed in 1876. Journal entries are missing for 1875, leaving one to wonder what quilts were pieced and quilted then. Early in 1876 when Lizzie finished Crowfoot, she was busy piecing on an **Ocean Wave** quilt and other small quilts for the little bed in addition to the **Pieced Brickwork** quilt, which would have been quick and easy to piece and quilt. As you read below, you will find Lizzie at work on several projects just like many quilters today.

1876

February 1st
very cool morning and quite a norther blowing - The menfolks hauling some dirt from the cow lot and putting it in the garden – I put in a worsted quilt to day and quilted some – it is peaced brick work

9th
Johny very sick yesterday – the Dr did not get here until this morning and he was considerably better. This is a pleasant day – I quilted some on the new quilt in the East room I have not yet got out my other one – in my room – but am quilting in the new room to keep Johny company

March 11th
An old Pedlar called this morning and talked us into buying some things - I would be glad another would not come in five years – I hemed 4 handkerchiefs and this eve fixed a lining and put in a quilt for the little bed

September 11th
Mended some and marked some things for Johnie and in the evening went to Plano to get a suit of clothes for him – as he is expecting to start school in a few days at Add Ran College in Hood county

20th
Cooked dinner to day and Martha washed I sewed some in the evening but don't remember what I made – Grass-hoppers by the millions

October 5th
To day I spun 8 cuts of yarn and reeled I a hundred and 20 threads to the cut – I also doubled a couple of brooches and have knit a right smart while I was resting – pretty good days work for an old clumsy woman If I do say it myself

7th
to day we all went to the grove to hunt grapes, pecans and walnuts – we stayed all day ...we had a nice time and the little boys were delighted

November 1st
I must cut some work and clean up my machine and get to sewing for I have a heap to do - later I finished a gown for myself

continued on page 70

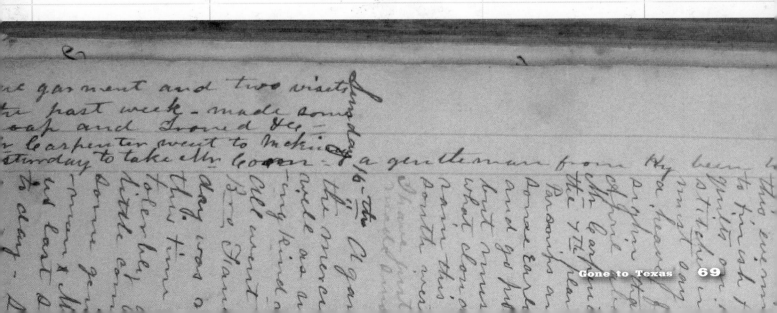

1876 continued

December 10th I sent Jeff to Mas with a small cake as it is her birth day – she is 75 years old to day

18th We have been married 25 years to day and we had calculated to celebrate the day with what is called a silver wedding

27th Day bright and clear – snow melting some little at Eleven o'clock – several stiring around this morning – I wish I was able to go to see ma I have not seen her for some time – and I would love to see her as well as other women for I have not seen one for two weeks – except for the negro girl Martha – and I do get so tired of nothing but men and boys – some half dozen men or more here already this morning – hope they make themselves scarce before I have to go about dinner – I will close now and try to do a little work – how I wish Ma would come

I have made in the year 1876 120 garments – peaced 3 quilts – quilted 3 – spun 15 cuts of stocking yarn – Also knit 16 pairs of stocking and socks – and done an abundance of mending I also done my house work or cooking 5 or 6 weeks – was sick in bed about one month – or nearly so – I attended church about 45 times – know not how many visits I made – but did many other things not set down here

Pieced Brickwork

1876
64" X 76"

MADE BY SONJA KRAUS
QUILTED BY SHERI MECOM

BLOCKS 4" x 8" FINISHED
AND 4" SQUARE FINISHED

Fabrics

1 1/8 yard brown floral.

4 1/2 yards assorted prints and plaids in 1/4 yard or 1/2 yard pieces.

5 1/4 yards backing in fabric of your choice.

5/8 yard binding in fabric of your choice to match the top.

Cutting

From the assorted prints and plaids, cut:

143 – 4 1/2" x 8 1/2" rectangles. Some prints may be used more than others.

18 – 4 1/2" squares.

Quilt top assembly

Pieced Brickwork is made from two alternating rows of rectangles and squares sewn into strips the width of the quilt. You may wish to use a design wall or to lay out all the rectangles and squares on the floor before sewing to be sure placement is to your liking.

To make Row A, arrange 8 rectangles in a random, yet pleasing row. Stitch the row together as shown, pressing to one side. Make 10 rows.

To make Row B, arrange 7 rectangles in a random yet pleasing row. Add 1 square to the ends of each row. Stitch the row together as shown, pressing to one side. Make 9 rows.

To assemble the top, stitch row to row alternating the two rows. Press seams all in one direction.

Finishing

Pieced Brickwork is quilted in an all-over meandering feather design.

Bind in the fabric of your choice.

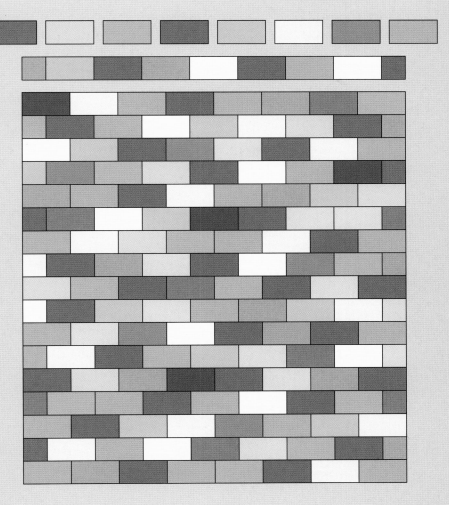

Ocean Wave

A full size Ocean Wave quilt requires a great deal of piecing. As you read the following entries you will notice that not only did Lizzie make one but so did her mother. Could they have shared fabrics? With so much family nearby this could have been a normal practice among the sisters and sisters-in-law, too.

1876

January 17th
I am working on my Ocean Waves quilt today – All well as common

27th a book agent called this morning – Mr C subscribed to a book – some of the boys are plowing – Mr Grady sharpening nails – I made a pair of drawers – molded some candles I and Mr Carpenter rode out on the pararie this eve

February 7th
This morning I quilted some – in the evening I and Martha picked the geese – Martha White came down this evening and I sewed a little for her on the machine – she in turn helped us pick geese

9th Johny very sick yesterday – the Dr did not get here until this morning and he was considerably better. This is a pleasant day – I quilted some on the new quilt in the East room I have not yet got out my other one – in my room – but am quilting in the new room to keep Johny company

23rd after dinner I got behind Mr C and rode up to mas as he went to Plano – worked some on my quilt Ocean Waves

26th cook and clean up and then cook again – quilted some little in the evening and got out my worsted quilt – sewed a few seed in the evening and mended some

March 1st
This was a tolerably pretty day some half dozen women here to help me quilt – and also some men here for dinner

2nd After getting breakfast and fixing up the men's dinners and cleaning up generally, I hemed a quilt and in the evening I went to see Ma a while – peaced a little on my quilt Ocean Wave

3rd This morning I concluded to do a big days work on the quilt that has been in so long but before I had fully finished my mornings work the dentist Dye came and went to work at pulling out some of my teeth – which was by no means a pleasant job for me, after that I prepared dinner for him and Mr C and in the evening I cut out some quilt peaces

15th I quilted on the small worsted quilt I put in yesterday

20th this is indeed quite a cold morning – some snow – and freezing all the while – boys hauling hay – I hemed a new quilt and mended some finished a pair of socks for Jeff

22nd I quilted and got out my quilt, some men are here this evening with a patent bee hive – we are having a hive transferred and some honey taken out – the gentlemen remained all night

24th bad morning – the children went to school – but came home again they did not stay long enough for the teacher to get there - John and Jeff went on Elm to hunt and fish – I finished peacing my ocean waves quilt today and mended some.

continued on page 78

Ocean Wave

1876
30" SQUARE

MADE AND QUILTED BY BETSY CHUTCHIAN

Fabrics

24 – 5" squares of assorted light prints, could use several charm packs.

24 – 5" squares of assorted dark prints, could use several charm packs.

1/2 yard medium value print for setting fabric.

1/2 yard brown print to match the quilt top for border.

1/3 yard brown print to match quilt top for binding.

1 yard for backing.

Cutting

From each 5" square, cut:
4 – 2 1/2" squares to total 192 squares.
Of these, select 16 light and 16 dark squares. Trim them to 2 3/8" and cut again diagonally once to equal 64 triangles. These triangles will be used in Blocks C, F, G, H and I.

From the setting fabric, cut:
1 – 7 1/4" square, cut again diagonally twice.
2 – 4" squares, cut again diagonally once. *Note*: These are oversized just a bit for trimming upon completion.
5 – 4 3/4" squares.

From the border fabric, cut:
4 – 3 1/2" strips by the width of fabric.

Block assembly

Ocean Wave Cradle Quilt is made of 9 different blocks that when joined together form the ocean waves pattern. *Note*: Be careful not to stretch the bias when pressing these blocks.

Half-square triangle units

1 1/2" finished
Make 160.
Mix and match 2 1/2" light and dark squares to make half-square triangle units. Draw a diagonal line on the wrong side of each light print and stitch with a scant quarter-inch seam on each side of the drawn line.
Cut apart on drawn line.
Press seams to the dark print.
Trim to 2".

Block A

6" finished
Make 2.
Arrange 16 half-square triangle units to match the block diagram. Sew into rows. Join rows together. Press units in opposing directions then press rows in one direction. Note: As you join blocks in rows and then sew rows together, stagger seams to reduce bulk.

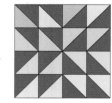

Block B

6" finished
Make 2.
Arrange 16 half-square triangle units to match the block diagram. Sew into rows. Join rows together. Press the same as Block A.

Block C

6" finished

Make 5.

Arrange 4 half-square triangle units, 4 light and 4 dark triangles and 1 setting square to match the block diagram. Press away from the half square triangle unit then press to setting square.

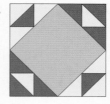

Block D

3"x 6" finished

Make 4.

Arrange 8 half-square triangle units to match the block diagram. Sew into rows. Join rows together. Press units in opposing directions then press rows in one direction.

Block E

3"x 6" finished

Make 4.

Arrange 8 half-square triangle units to match the block diagram. Sew into rows. Join rows together. Press units in opposing directions then press rows in one direction.

Block F

3" x 6" finished

Make 2.

Arrange 2 half-square triangle units, 2 light and 2 dark triangles and 1 large setting triangle to match the block diagram. Sew into rows. Join rows together. Press away from the half-square triangle units then press to the large triangle. Be careful not to stretch the bias when pressing.

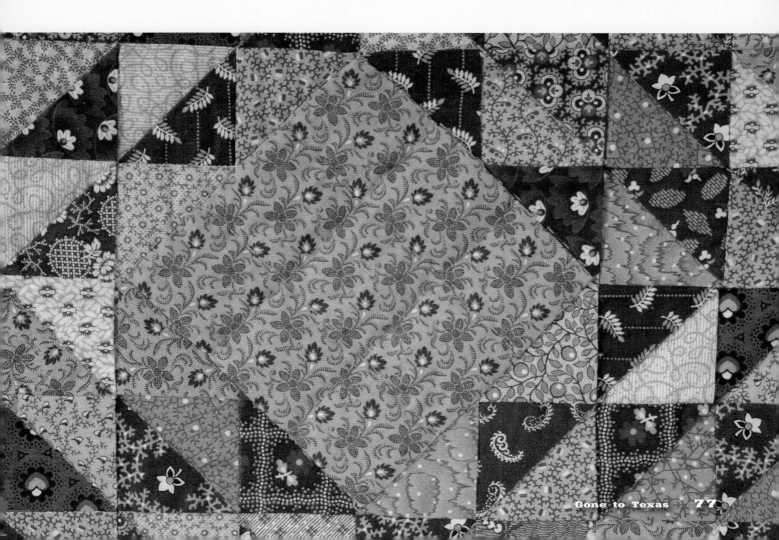

Block G

3"x 6" finished
Make 2.
Arrange 2 half-square triangle units, 2 light and 2 dark triangles and 1 large setting triangle to match the block diagram. Sew into rows. Join rows together. Press away from the half-square triangle units then press to the large triangle.

Block I

3" finished
Make 2.
Arrange 1 half-square triangle units, 2 light triangles and 1 small setting triangle to match the block diagram. Sew into rows. Join rows together. Press to small side triangles, then press unit to larger triangle.

Block H

3" finished
Make 2.
Arrange 1 half-square triangle units, 2 dark triangles and 1 small setting triangle to match the block diagram. Sew into rows. Join rows together. Press to small side triangles, then press unit to larger triangle.

1876 *continued from page 74*

continued from page 74

April 5th to day I made two pair of pillow slips for the pillows on the boys little bed I ribed them in calico and it took me a good while – this has been a very pretty day – our boys finished planting corn to day

May 13th I set at the sewing machine most all day – Made Bobbies coat and pants and was not at all well either

22nd Still feeling very poorly - I embroidered some little on a gown yoke – very sick at my stomach all day

June 4th Willies birth day – I am not feeling well enough to make him a cake – am sitting up very little to day – several lady friends to see me this evening – I was glad to see them company cheers me up so much

7th to day Mr Carpenter took me down to see sister Mary Brown and her new baby – she was well and so is the big fat boy

15th I went to mas and spent the day with her – helped her

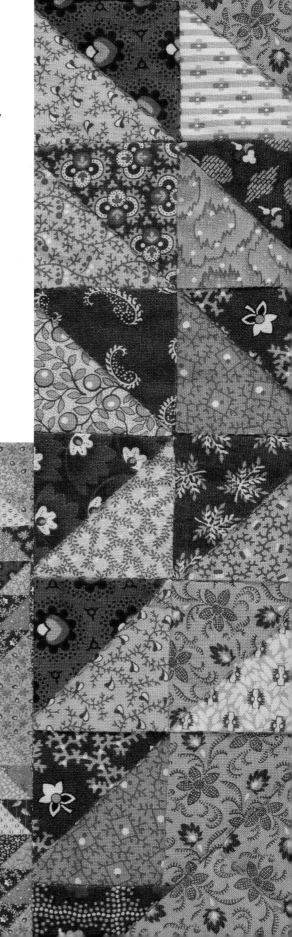

Quilt top assembly

Arrange blocks according to the diagram. Sew into rows. Join the rows together.

H	D	G	D	I
E	C	A	C	E
F	B	C	B	F
E	C	A	C	E
I	D	G	D	H

Borders

Measure your quilt top through the middle from top to bottom. Cut 2 lengths of the border strips to match your measurement. Sew to the sides of the quilt, pressing to the border.

Measure your quilt top again, through the middle from side to side. Cut 2 lengths of the border strips to match your measurement. Sew to the top and bottom of the quilt, pressing to the border.

Finishing

Ocean Wave is hand quilted in a grid across the alternate blocks and lines that follow the long side of the triangles.

Bind in fabric to match the quilt top.

1877

January 22nd "My little Mary Catherine was born on the 6th of January, 1877 very early on Saturday morning"

April 9th I went to Ma's to see Mary Lunsford she has a young babe – tis a boy and the biggest babe I think I ever saw – tis 3 days old and is larger than Mary at 3 months

December 31st I am in the habit of writing how many gar-ments I made in a year and this year I have only made about 95 -100- not near so many as common but I think does well considering my babys health and the attention that she required – I also knit about 8 or 10 pair of socks and stockings – but have peaced no quilts this year as I usialy do – but I do thank the Lord and my god this night that I have been enabled to do as much for our dear family as I have—

1878

January 8th The snow is not quite gone yet been 5 days since it fell - Mr C started yesterday morning with his mules for market – went east to Smith and adjoining counties

T Quilt

1877 and 1878 were hard years for Lizzie. Her eighth child, a little girl, was born in 1877 and lived 14 months. The baby took most of her time and attention. Realizing this, she worried that she was neglecting the rest of her family. A sense of normalcy returns in 1879.

You will notice that Lizzie said some called the T quilt, the Cross. The block does have that appearance, especially on point as I have set it. Double T is also a common name for this block.

– expect he will be gone two or three weeks perhaps longer Adelia Brown and Fannie Mathews spent the day with me – we have been working on a quilt for Ruth – she worked for me last summer – I have just fixed up the lining and Adelia will quilt it for me

10th Such an abundance of mud I don't think I ever saw so much mud before – I am scarcely doing anything these times but nursing and sweeping- and yesterday and to day I have been cooking as Lucy was washing – I fixed up the quilt for Ruth and sent it to Adelia – I tried to make a little soap and suceded poorly – I miss Mr Carpenter very much and think baby Mary does also – her birthday was 4 days ago – I weighed her and she weighed 12 pounds and has two teeth- she rests very poorly at night

17th I have been busy to day working on a quilt setting it together, Delia promised to quilt it for me – it is the Cross or some I believe call it the T

26th I went up to Willies and spent the day – Emma was peaceing a quilt and Willie was plowing- that make s the 3rd visit I have made since Mr C has been gone—It will be 3 weeks since he left…little Mary is not well to day and is crying so I must stop writing and take her – perhaps write on tomorrow

February 12th
This is a rather ugly day – raw wind from the south and cloudy – looks something like snow- Mr C is riding around looking after the stock – I have done but little as usial sewing on myself a calico dress this evening- dark brown with a small white flower – Baby is sleeping sweetly now so I will close and go to work – She don't seem very well to day

March 6th
Warm and cloudy- the boys to begin to plant corn- I want to make some more garden to day as I have not a great deal- bro Simon Lundsford is here painting the smoke house – most of us suffering with bad colds- Little Mary is also poorly with cold

(Mary Katie died March 14, 1878. The cause of death was never mentioned, but from the journals it appears that the baby was sickly from birth.)

March 17th
O Lord have mercy on us poor frail creatures – and help us to live as we ought before thee each day. Oh what a sadness is in my heart and on my breast – seems as if some heavy hand my bosom prest – our darling babe our dear Mary Katie is gone – yes gone from the trials and sorrows of Earth - Oh tis hard very hard to give her up and it seems as though I cant get reconciled to it and I will try to be reconciled to the Lords will – yet I loved her so very much. The world is beautiful to those that know not sorrow. For nature is putting on her most lovely robe the orchards are a lovely pink alternately spotted with light and deeper colored blossoms- and many of the fields and some of the prararies are covered with a carpet of delicate green – but our heart is sore – we cant enjoy the lovely sight to day for the image of my darling babe is almost constantly before my eyes and in my thoughts – if I did not have constant employment I could not stand it

continued on page 84

T Quilt

1878
58 1/2" X 79 3/4"

MADE BY BETSY CHUTCHIAN
QUILTED BY SHERI MECOM

BLOCKS 7 1/2" FINISHED

Fabrics

1 3/4 yards total of assorted light prints and shirting fabric, or 24 – 10" squares.

3 yards total of assorted dark prints, or 24 - fat eighths.

2 3/4 yards pink for setting squares and triangles.

1 yard brown print for border.

5/8 yard brown for binding.

5 yards print of your choice for backing.

Cutting

From assorted light prints, cut:
48 – 3 3/8" squares, cut again diagonally once (A).
48 – 3 3/4" squares, cut again diagonally twice (B).

From assorted dark prints, cut:
48 – 3 3/8" squares, cut again diagonally once (C).
192 – 2 1/8" squares, cut again diagonally once (D).
24 – 3" square for center (E).

From pink, cut:
15 – 8" squares for setting squares.

4 – 11 7/8" squares, cut again diagonally twice for side setting triangles.

2 – 6 1/4" squares, cut again diagonally once for setting corners.

8 – 4 1/2" wide strips x width of fabric for borders.

From brown, cut:
7 – 4 1/2" wide strips by the width of fabric for border.

T block assembly

7 1/2" finished
Make 24 blocks

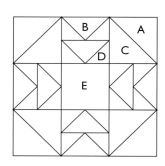

To make 1 block
Each block is made of 4 half-square triangle units, 4 double flying geese units and one 3" square.

Half-square triangle units

2 1/2" square finished
Make 4

Make the half-square triangle units by sewing 1 dark C triangle and 1 light A triangle together with a scant one-quarter seam allowance. Press to the dark.

Double flying geese units

2 1/2" square finished unit (1 flying geese unit is 1 1/4" x 2 1/2" finished).
Make 4

Make the double flying geese units by sewing 2 dark D triangles to one B light triangle as shown in diagram. Press to the dark, being careful not to stretch the bias. Repeat with 2 more D triangles and 1 B triangle. Join these two units together to complete the double flying geese unit.

1878 *continued*

March 26th
Mr C and myself went to Dallas last week the first time I have been there in 14 or 15 years – quite a change in that time – yes changes in many things and many ways – we went on the cars (train) and came back the same way – a rather tiresome trip leaving early and getting home at midnight

April 21st
made 6 garments the past week We went to John Browns and spent the day with sister – she has quite a houseful of healthy interesting children 4 girls and 2 boys – the youngest 4 months and ever so much stronger and stouter than our little darling at 14 months – it seems a wonder we kept her as long as we did

May 1st
Wednesday Mr C myself and the little boys went to McKinney Saturday on the train as they had never riden the cars before – we came back in the waggon with Willie and Emma as they also went up – Monday I made Jeff a pair of pants - Tuesday got dinner and batted some cotton and put in a lounge quilt and quilted some – I want to quilt a goodeal to day – so I must get to it

July 20th
I have been busied canning some tomatoes and making some catsup and cleaning up and have a goodeal yet to do this evening – want to make some peach butter – also bake some light bread and sweep and clean up which is my Saturday work especially – the boys have gone to Plano this eve to play base ball with the Plano Club – the little boys have been gathering me some peaches

29th
we witnessed the impressive and grand sight of a total eclipse of the sun – such a scene I never expected to witness or do I ever expect to witness it again – It was very impressive and made one feel like they were almost standing in the presence of Jehovah –

December 31st
I must now count up and see how much work I have done this year or how many articles I have made as is my usial practice – I have done my cooking and other house work about six months in this year and most of the washing and Ironing with some of the mens help to work the washing machine-

During the past year I have made 84 articles – Peaced about 3 quilts - quilted 3 quilts and one comfort – Knit and footed about 12 pair of socks and stockings – attended Sunday School 25 times Social worship and preaching about 30 times – done a great deal of mending – not very many visits except to see the sick about 30 or more times – So ends my work for the year 1878 – May the Lord bless my labors

1879

September 5th
My dear old journal I have sadly neglected you of late – I have been busily engaged of late with other matters that you have scarcely been thought of...will close now and commence dinner – I am chief cook or the only cook

15th
Mr C has gone to Plano – Jeff is plowing – John and Bobbie are picking cotton – I have done nothing to day but house work and I have not been very well – however I must try directly to finish a pair of pants that I commenced last week – for I have a great deal of sewing to do and some quilts to quilt which I fear wont get done for it seems I cant get any one to help with the cooking and I cant do much else when I do that and the starching and the Ironing

December 31st
I am in the habit of setting down how many garments I make during the year – this year I have done my house work 9 ½ months and can't have as many as usial – I have made 100 or perhaps a few over – and have peaced one quilt and quilted four ---besides much mending and knitting – I am doing my house work at present – I believe I feel better doing it than not – I do not take enough exercise when I do not do any house work – I will close and say good bye to another year perhaps the last I may ever see the close of – if so tis well for I am in the hands of Him who doeth all things well - Farewell

Block assembly

To make the T block, lay out the 4 half-square triangle units, the 4 double flying geese units and the plain square as shown in the assembly diagram.
Sew into rows.
Join the rows.

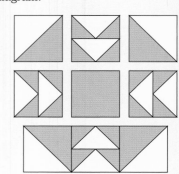

Quilt top assembly

Lay out the T blocks, setting squares, setting triangles and corners in diagonal rows as shown in the assembly diagram. Stitch rows together. Press to setting pieces.

Borders

Add two borders; the first border is brown and the outer border is pink. Add sides first, then top and bottom.

Measure your quilt top through the center from top to bottom. Join lengths of the 4 1/2" wide brown border strips to match your measurement. Sew to the sides of the quilt, pressing to the border.

Measure your quilt top again, through the center from side to side. Join lengths of the 4 1/2" wide brown border strips to match your measurement. Sew to the top and bottom of the quilt, pressing to the border.

Repeat the process with the outer 4 1/2" wide pink border.

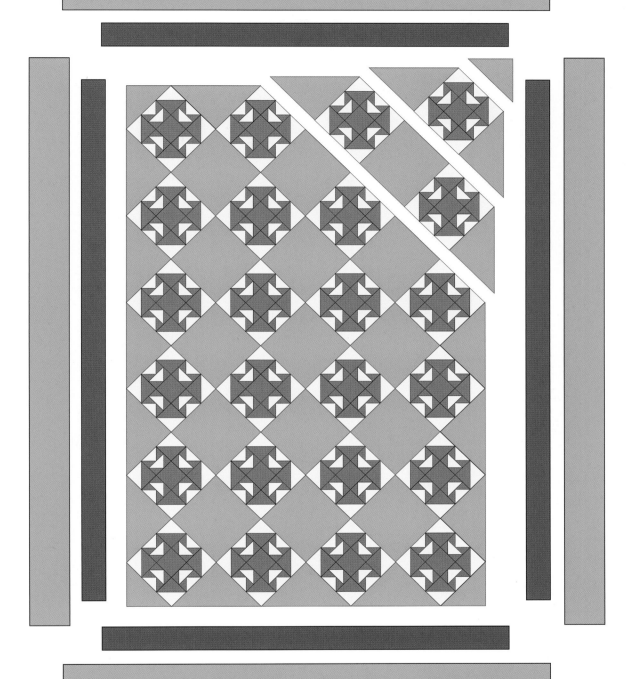

Finishing

The T quilt is quilted in parallel diagonal lines, a feather design in the brown border and chevrons in the pink border.
Bind with pink or brown fabric.

Lone Star

Lizzie died in 1882 after a short illness. The last years of her life were spent just as the previous had been – quilting, sewing and tending to her domestic duties. The Lone Star quilt, also known as Bethlehem Star, was one of her last completed quilts. One can only wonder how many projects she left unfinished.

1881

January 7th made about 3 articles this week – I have also finished a quilt – The Lone Star

April 2nd this week I have been quilting- put in my Lone Star on last Tuesday – have not got very much done on it yet

7th I feel there is no rest for my head, headache all night but not as severe this morning as last night - Monday I mended some and planted some flower seed – and in the evening made me an apron- Tuesday I quilted some and wrote a letter to Gipson

13th I have been quilting this week Ida helped me Saturday and Monday

19th sister Smith came down and we got out the quilt I had in – I will set down the things I got at Plano saturday the 16th Calico 20yds $1.40,

20yds cotton check 1.40, 5yds cotton-ade 1.25, 2 yds slate colored shambra .50, 5 yds Jack edging 1.75, 1 hat for Eddie .75

30th Last night Jeff got in from Hood county – he came on the train and walked home, got here at 2 o'clock – Gipson came through in there old buggy – and Loula came on the train with Jeff – I was glad to see them all again

December 27th I have made for this year 120 garments, doing my cooking and my house work all the year

1882

January 9th Mr Carpenter is gone to McKinney summoned to serve on the grand jury – the little boys are at school and I am entirely alone – I put in a quilt and ate a snack of dinner and now will set in to quilting – will close now and get to work at my quilt – which is run on lining and don't require much quilting

17th I got out my quilt on Friday I have also done some mending and a goodeal of knitting

30th I have not done much settled work I have sewed someone a quilt made of wolen goods, mostly old pants

February 1st I will try to work on the yarn quilt I have on hand

9th Thursday Since the last date I finished the yarn quilt and began another one and have also been working on a calico one and also on my worsted quilt

August 28th

[Lizzie's last entry]

I will try to note a few items this evening although I am busy yet I have not communicated with my journal for some

cont. on page 93

Poor Bird

Lone Star

1881
71" X 71"

MADE BY BETSY CHUTCHIAN
QUILTED BY SHERI MECOM

Fabrics

2 yards light print or solid background for star and sawtooth border.

1 1/4 yards red fabric for sawtooth border and binding.

3 3/4 yards brown print – 1 1/2 yards for inner border, 2 1/4 yards for outer border.

5 yards backing pieced to measure 79" square.

For strip sets (diamond sections):

1/4 yard brown (A)

1/3 yard red (B)

1/2 yard pink (C)

2/3 yard green (D)

3/4 yard blue (E)

1/2 yard gold (F)

Cutting

For strip sets, cut from width of fabric:

2 – 2" wide strips (A)

4 – 2" wide strips (B)

6 – 2" wide strips (C)

8 – 2" wide strips (D)

10 – 2" wide strips (E)

6 – 2" wide strips (F)

From background fabric, cut:

1 – 20 1/4" square, cut diagonally twice for star background.

4 – 14" squares for star background.

36 – 4" squares for sawtooth border.

From the red fabric, cut:

36 – 4" squares for sawtooth border.

From the 2 1/4 yard cut of brown print, cut:

4 – 7 1/2" wide strips x the length of fabric for the outer border.

Reserve the 1 1/2 yard cut of brown print for the Inner Border. Instructions for cutting are detailed below with Inner Border instructions.

Strip set assembly

Sew 2 strip sets of each group as shown, offsetting the beginning of each strip by 1 1/2" as shown.

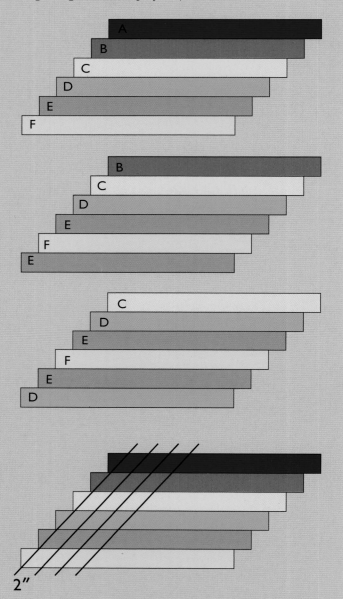

2"

Carefully cut at 2" intervals using the 45 degree angle on a long wide ruler. *Note*: take your time and trim if angle of cut is not exactly 45 degrees, readjust and resume cutting. Be as accurate as possible.

Diamond assembly

Sew strips together in pairs, pinning seam intersections carefully. Be sure to offset edges by a quarter-inch as shown to ensure the proper seam allowance. Before stitching, carefully open up the strips and take a look to make sure the seams are lined up correctly.

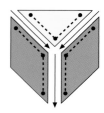

Sew 8 diamond units as shown.

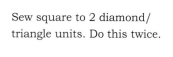

Lone Star assembly

Sew diamond units in pairs with a side triangle. This is a Y seam construction, but sew in three separate steps. Do not cross seam allowance at beginning or end. Sew from outside in to middle as shown backstitching at beginning points and ending points. Dots indicate quarter-inch seam and where to backstitch. *Note:* This is different from traditional Y-seam construction.

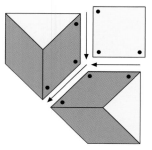

Sew square to 2 diamond/ triangle units. Do this twice.

Sew large pieced units together then add final 2 corners.

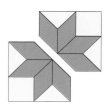
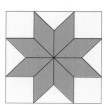

Inner border

In order for the Sawtooth border to fit evenly, the inner border must finish to 51" once sewn on the Lone Star block. To determine the width your inner border should be, measure your Lone Star block through the middle from top to bottom and side to side. Subtract the half-inch seam allowance and note that measurement. Subtract it from 51. Divide that number by two and add the half-inch seam allowance back on to get the width you should cut your inner border.

For example, the Lone Star block shown in the photograph measured 43 inches, finished. 51" – 43" = 8". Divide 8" by 2 to get 4". Add a half-inch seam allowance to get 4 1/2" wide inner borders.

Once you have determined your border width, cut the brown fabric that width x your Lone Star block measurement. The side borders for the example shown were cut 4 1/2" x 43 1/2".

For the top and bottom borders, cut 2 strips your width x 51 1/2". The example shown was cut 4 1/2"" x 51 1/2".

The top should now measure 51 1/2" square.

Sawtooth border

Make 72 half-square triangle units. Draw a diagonal line on wrong side of 36 – 4" background squares. Pair the background squares with 36 – 4" red squares right sides together.

Sew one-quarter inch on each side of drawn line. Cut apart on drawn lines. Press seam to red. Trim triangle units to 3 1/2".

Sew 2 side borders of 17 triangle units each. Be sure to make the triangles point in the desired direction. See assembly diagram on page 92 for guidance. Sew to sides of star.

Sew top and bottom borders of 19 triangle units. Sew to top and bottom of star.

The quilt top should measure 57 1/2".

1882 *continued from page 89*

continued from page 89

time so I must say a few things this evening as I expect to start on a trip to Hood County tomorrow and perhaps will not have another opportunity of writing in my book for some weeks. ...we expect to be 8 or 10 days on the road with sheep – as Mr Carpenter desires to take our about 250 to put on his ranch – I and the little boys are just going to help him and to try to make the trip more pleasant for him...Jeff will be at home to see to things

Lizzie passed away September 24, 1882, a few weeks short of her 50th birthday. According to her obituary, she got sick with dysentery on the trip to Hood County and died shortly after returning home. Robert continued writing in Lizzie's journal for one year. In her treasured book he wrote of his sorrow and loneliness, the health of their family and friends, the weather, the crops, the church meetings and so forth just as she had recorded since 1857. Robert mourned for a year then married Nellie Tipton and they had one son, Gano.

Robert writes on November 16, 1882 that "Jeff has gone to Dr Shelburne's to recite for him. He has commenced to read medicine and I hope that he will make a good doctor and a good man."

Jeff, my great-grandfather, continued to study medicine in Kentucky. There he met and married Florence Gough, granddaughter of John Mathews, Lizzie's brother. They returned to Texas, sold his farm to his father moved to Little Elm, Texas where he began to practice medicine.

Jeff and Florence had 6 children, the eldest Edgar died very young. My grandmother, Ethel Elizabeth was born December 10, 1889. She graduated from college in Denton, Texas and married John Carter in 1908. To their union was born three children, Ethelyn, John Jr., and my mother, Florence Marie, April 12, 1920.

Outer border

Measure your quilt top through the middle from top to bottom. Cut 2 lengths of 7 1/2" wide brown print strips to match your measurement. Sew to the sides of the quilt, pressing to the border.

Measure your quilt top again, through the middle from side to side. Cut 2 lengths of 7 1/2" wide brown print strips to match your measurement. Sew to the top and bottom of the quilt, pressing to the border.

Finishing.

Lone Star is quilted using a combination of feathered wreaths in the background fabrics and a feathered border. The diamonds are quilted using complementary straight lines to contrast the feathers.

Bind in red.

The antique quilts

Because none of Lizzie's quilts have survived the years, I used many period quilts as inspiration when recreating her quilts for this book. Some of these have stories as fascinating as those for Lizzie's quilts.

Gone To Texas, *page 15.*

This quilt (on the bed) is a fabric lovers quilt! Composed of more than 2,000 pieces, it showcases hundreds of different fabrics dating from the mid-1800s. Some of the individual blocks alone contain 40 or more different fabrics. My reproduction has a mere 2,139 pieces, while the original has 2,200. (For more about the antique Gone To Texas quilt see page 8.)

Soldiers Parade, *page 15.*

The antique quilt (over the foot of the bed), dated 1862 on its back side, is a Birds in the Air variation. While the printed fabrics have severely deteriorated, the magnificent hand quilting remains as stunning as ever. When examining this quilt for the book, I remembered reading that Lizzie and Mrs. Bush "went up to see the soldiers encamped up on White Rock – we saw them parade and exercising their sword" – September 30, 1861. The strippy setting of the many triangles made me think of soldiers marching, and that's how it got its name. The quit is owned by Denice Lipscomb of Waxahachie, Texas.

Crowfoot, *page 62.*

This piece of a quilt top (over the foot of the bed) has quite a mystery attached to it! I found this quilt top some years ago in Fort Worth, Texas. Not too long after, I attended a workshop by Terry Thompson in Lawrence, Kansas. There, in Terry's stacks of quilts for class, was the other half of my quilt top (shown on the bed)! After examining both quilt tops, it is obvious they are sections of the exact same quilt. How half ended up in Kansas and half in Texas, we'll never know. They are shown together here for the first time.